W9-CTX-269

WINNING THE DISCIPLINE DEBATES

Winning
the
Discipline
Debates

Dr. Ray Coaches Parents
to Make Discipline
Less Frequent,
Less Frustrating,
and More Consistent

DR. RAY GUARENDI

SERVANT
BOOKS

PUBLISHED BY FRANCISCAN MEDIA
Cincinnati, Ohio

Cover design by Candle Light Studios
Book design by Mark Sullivan

LIBRARY OF CONGRESS CATALOGING-IN-PUBLICATION DATA
Guarendi, Raymond.
Winning the discipline debates : Dr. Ray coaches parents / Ray Guarendi.
p. cm.
ISBN 978-1-61636-437-3 (alk. paper)
1. Discipline of children. 2. Child rearing. 3. Parenting. I. Title.
HQ770.4.G824 2013
649'.64—dc23
2012036647

ISBN 978-1-61636-437-3
Copyright © 2013, Dr. Ray Guarendi. All rights reserved.

Published by Servant Books, an imprint of
Franciscan Media
28 W. Liberty St.
Cincinnati, OH 45202
www.Franciscan Media.org

Printed in the United States of America.
Printed on acid-free paper.
13 14 15 16 17 5 4 3 2 1

To Mom and Pop
My first book was to you
when you were here.
This one's for you
in your hereafter.

CONTENTS

ACKNOWLEDGMENTS

Thank you to:

Claudia Volkman, director of product development at Servant Books, who kindly contacted me, introduced herself, and promptly asked what I might have going in the way of book ideas. Always pleasant to work with, your every-step-of-the-way guidance was invaluable.

Misty Woodrum, for your tireless typing and retyping of my re-re-reedits, along with your willingness to learn to translate a second language—my nearly illegible handwritten manuscript.

Randi, my wife, who is ever willing to carry far more than her share of the family load every time I write a book about family. Your instinctive wisdom marvels me more with each book.

Andrew, Hannah, Jonathan, Joanna, Sarah, Samuel, James, Mary, Peter, and Elizabeth. You continue to give me more than enough material to keep writing.

INTRODUCTION

No end is in sight to the books proposing the psychologically correct ways to communicate with children. (Unfortunately, the kids have no interest in reading them.) Each expert puts forth his notions of how to talk to children, with children, about children, near children. In our ten-child household, my wife and I would be happy knowing how to talk louder than children.

The proliferation of books has led me to wonder if all their advice—routinely contradictory—is a reflection of a frustration at trying to consistently connect with a being who, by his very nature, does not view the world with adult eyes. This is not to say that some styles aren't better than others. And certainly, some kids respond well to the very same approach that other kids would either laugh at or chew into pieces. It is to say that there are no foolproof formulas for persuading young people to think or act along the lines we'd like, at least not in the near term. Maybe by the time they have their own children, or grandchildren. Expert-driven ideas may sound swell on paper, but in the real world they run headlong into a most unpredictable creature—a child.

Am I advising that you take a page from the kids' book and ignore guidance? No. For one thing, that would also include mine. For another, it's not so much the assortment of advice that confuses; it's affording any one piece of advice too much status. It is hearing it as the "proven" path to happy, psychologically well-wrapped children. The truth speaks with a different voice: No one communication size fits all kids or, for that matter, stops all kids' fits.

While some say common sense is not so common, most loving parents have a healthy reservoir from which to draw. Good sense and instincts remain the foundation of solid parenting. All advice—expert and otherwise—is best viewed through one's personal lens: How well does this suit me, my family, and my morals?

With this as my guide, I propose some ideas for talking to children—more specifically, talking to children in a confident discipline voice. Not that my suggestions are distinctly mine. Other expert types also recommend them. More critical, though, is the fact that these ideas have evolved and endured in the accumulated wisdom of countless parents over countless generations. The equation is elegantly simple: Good words plus good actions equal great teaching.

Winning the Discipline Debates presents everyday discipline scenarios, with children from preschool to late teen. Wives might wonder if any of these could apply to raising husbands. Not really, other than certain select preschool ones.

In each scenario everybody gets a chance to talk—parents, kids, and me. The parents say and do the stuff of discipline—both the effective and the not so. The kids provide standard resistances and comebacks. I, the ever-present bystander, observe the whole interplay, offering words and techniques to defuse discord as well as sharpen the parents' discipline skills.

Anything I contribute is for your consideration, to accept or reject, to select or neglect. Choose what makes the most sense to you, what is most in line with your particular parenting aims. My aim is to make your discipline less wordy, less frustrating, less frequent, and more definite.

I'll write the script. You read it, acting out what you think best. Just don't let the kids peruse it before you do.

CHAPTER 1

Who's Asking?

Actors: Mom; five-year-old Taylor
Scene: Preschool
Time: Pick-up

PROLOGUE
Questions may sound like a nice way to speak with authority, but their actual effect is to put authority in question.

Mom: Hey, Taylor. How was school today?
Taylor: Good.
Mom: What did you do?
Taylor: Some stuff.
Mom: Did you have fun?
Taylor: Uh-huh.
Dr. Ray: If one has any question as to whether Taylor is a boy or girl, it is answered. Despite Mom's noble attempts to ask open-ended questions, the kind designed to encourage children to "share," Taylor responds in basic little-boy style—one word, maybe two in a moment of explosive self-revelation. Were Taylor the typical little girl, I might not get the chance to talk until three pages from now.
Mom: Well, Taylor, are you ready to go now? Let's get your coat, OK? Do you want to say good-bye to your teacher?
Dr. Ray: Mom is shifting the nature of her questions. No longer seeking Taylor's conversation, she is now seeking his cooperation.

Taylor: No, I'm not ready to go now. It's not OK for us to get my coat. And I don't feel like saying good-bye to my teacher.

Dr. Ray: All right, I put those words in Taylor's mouth. As are most kids, he is too savvy to give so blatantly blunt a retort. But I suspect some such thoughts are percolating in his head. Mom is striving to sound less authoritative, more "nice," conveying a "We're all in this together, OK?" mentality. Of course, if her queries move Taylor, then the goals are achieved: smooth transition to the car, potential scene averted. If not, Mom is left with only a couple of avenues. One, ask again, in a more entreating tone, hoping to evoke Taylor's agreement. Or two, move directly to clear statements.

Mom: Taylor, get your coat, please, and tell your teacher good-bye.

Dr. Ray: One can be both definite and pleasant. *Please* is a form of amicable request, but it is not an open-ended plea for cooperation. *Please* can introduce most parenting directives yet still convey calm resolve. The message resides in the demeanor: I'm asking for your cooperation, but I do expect it.

Taylor: Is it time to go already? Where did I put my coat? Which one of these people is my teacher?

Mom: C'mon, Taylor. Your sister is in the car and hasn't talked to me in almost four minutes. She is probably bursting to talk.

EPILOGUE

Question discipline can get good results, provided both you and the child understand that the matter is not open to discussion. The real question is: Is it better to ask first and then become more direct as needed? Or is it better, nicer even, to begin by being direct? I think you know the answer to that, don't you?

CHAPTER 2

Night Daze

Actors: Mom; Dad; four-year-old Wakefield
Scene: Wakefield's bedroom; Mom and Dad's bedroom; kitchen
Time: Bedtime; middle of the night; next day

PROLOGUE

Life is wired backward. We grown-ups desperately fight to sleep more. Little kids desperately fight to sleep less.

Wakefield: Just one more story, OK, Mom? Read me the one about the snake that likes cupcakes.

Mom: I think we've had enough for tonight. We've already read two stories. And we brushed our teeth, said our prayers, and gave kisses. That means it's time to sleep.

Wakefield: But I'm not sleepy. Just one more story, and I'll be tired.

Dr. Ray: It's the "bedtime ritual," as some experts have dubbed it. Parents are advised to set up a standard, predictable routine. Doing so will ready the toughest of bed battlers to transition from a period of "activity" to one of "inactivity" every night.

My guess is that most of these experts don't have preschoolers, or if they do, they can't get them to bed without a fuss, ritual or no. In my experience, about 3 percent of little kids will be moved to stillness after some sort of routine. The other 97 percent will reserve their most energetic arousal for after the ritual.

"Just one more story, and I'll be tired." Maybe, if it's an unabridged recitation of *War and Peace*. In Latin.

Mom: We'll do more stories tomorrow. Right now it's bedtime.

Wakefield: But I'm really not sleepy. Don't go yet. Stay with me until I go to sleep.

Mom: You need to learn how to go to sleep without me lying here with you every night. It's time for you to be a big boy and sleep by yourself in your bed. Good night. (Kisses Wakefield and heads for the kitchen.)

Dr. Ray: If Mom has been nightly lying in bed with Wakefield, she has become entrapped in her own ritual. Further, the more of those nights, the more prolonged Wakefield's resistance when Mom tries to retreat alone to her own bed.

The "big boy" appeal can succeed with little boys, unless it collides with a rival appeal—the drive to stay out of the "big boy" bed.

Wakefield (forty-seven seconds later, walking somberly into the kitchen): Mommy, I can't sleep. Can I stay here with you?

Mom (through semi-clenched teeth, walking Wakefield back up to his room): Come on. Let's go back to bed. You just need to lie still, and then you'll fall asleep. Do you want your stuffed tiger to cuddle with? Here, I'll cover you up and leave the hall light on.

Dr. Ray: Mom is pulling out all her stops: the escort to bed, the "strong" stuffed animal companion, the overhead light. She's still hoping to persuade, to make sleep a pleasant experience. (If only little kids had our grown-up love for sleep.)

Persuasion, which includes addressing every creative excuse, can soothe, but generally it will only do so in the first several minutes. Night after night of struggle, or even an endless one-night struggle, is a pretty clear sign that nothing but firmness is going to settle anyone. The child's unspoken response is, I don't want to go to bed, no matter how good you try to make it sound.

Wakefield: Stay here, Mommy, OK? Please? Then I'll go to sleep.

Mom: I can't right now. I have things to do. I'll be going to bed pretty soon too. Then we'll both be asleep. Now, you stay in bed, OK? (Leaving for the kitchen.)

Wakefield: I love you, Mommy, and I'll miss you.

Mom: I'll miss you too. Bedtime now, OK?

Dr. Ray: As we noted a few pages ago, when a parent follows a request or command with "OK?" she doesn't really mean "OK?" She's just trying to be nice about it.

Mom could have told Wakefield exactly what she would do should he get out of bed again, but apparently she is still waiting for him to be negotiable. Clinging to the possibility of a peaceful evening, Mom returns to the kitchen.

Wakefield (returning to the kitchen ninety-three seconds later): Mommy, I'm scared. I need you to protect me.

Mom: Your little light is on, and so is the hall light. Now, you get back in your bed.

Dr. Ray: Had Wakefield claimed fear earlier, Mom might have given him a little more credibility. With her patience thinning, she is less inclined to hear much more.

Commonly preschoolers will voice some measure of fear at the core of their resistance. How much is genuine and how much is manipulation can be hard to sort out. Nevertheless, after a parent has reassured, put extra lights on, prayed for protection, placed a port-a-john in the bedroom—all with little success, especially after nightly replays—she is forced to take a stand.

For both big and little people, moving beyond an irrational fear routinely involves living through the fear and realizing that all the imagined bad things didn't happen. Even if some bit of fear is mixed with a child's resistance, almost always it fades when he finds out—often against his will—that there is nothing to fear. Now Wakefield, after nine minutes of crying, reenters the kitchen.

Mom: Now why are you crying?

Wakefield: I told you. I'm really scared. I think I saw a monster outside. And I have to go to the potty too.

Mom: You went potty right before you went to bed. But if you have to go again, make it quick, and then you go straight back to bed.

Wakefield: OK.

Dr. Ray: Yeah, right.

Mom (nine minutes later, checking on Wakefield's bathroom progress): Wakefield, what are you doing in here? I think you're stalling. Let's go. Back in bed now! You didn't even have to go.

Wakefield: Uh-huh. I'm just not done yet.

Mom (grabbing Wakefield's wrist): Well, you're done now. And I'm taking you to bed. And if you get out again, you'll be in trouble. Now, good night, for the last time.

Wakefield: Mommy, please, just a little bit, lie with me. I'll be quiet, and then I'll go to sleep. Please.

Mom (near her breaking point, wanting peace at any price): All right. I'll stay here, but just for a little bit until you get tired.

Dr. Ray: Nine minutes later Mom is dozing and Wakefield is smacking his stuffed tiger. When his elbow bangs Mom in the face, she startles awake and stumbles toward her bedroom, forgetting about her chores and desperately craving sleep.

If this were the first, the second, or even the third night of Wakefield's bedtime dance, one might acknowledge Mom's efforts to reassure and compromise. But if this is standard routine—and by the sounds of it, it is—then Mom needs a different tack. Let's go back to Wakefield's first appearance in the kitchen.

Wakefield: Mommy, I can't sleep. Can I stay here with you?

Mom: No, you can't. And I told you to stay in bed. So now please go to the corner, and you'll stay there until I think you're ready to stay in bed.

Dr. Ray: What if Wakefield refuses the corner? We'll answer that shortly, after Mom is asleep.

For now, the first step toward rest for all is to early and clearly place a consequence upon leaving the bed or nagging from it. Such is not being rigid; it is being kind. Nobody benefits from a marathon contest of wills, especially when both parties need to sleep, one now, the other later.

Let's move to a later scene of the original scenario.

Wakefield (1:45 AM, walking into Mom and Dad's room, standing next to the bed): Mom… Mom… Mommy, I can't sleep 'cause I'm scared.

Mom: Wakefield, please go back to bed. I told you there's nothing to be afraid of.

Wakefield: But I can't sleep, 'cause I saw something on the wall.

Dad (awakening): Eve, just let him get in bed with us. I've got to get up early, and we can't keep messing with him all night.

Mom: OK, Wakefield, but this is the last time we're going to let you do this.

Dr. Ray: If Mom doesn't realize it now, she will twenty-four hours from now: She just invited another bout of the same hassle tomorrow, and likely for more nights after that. And while the imbroglio might be over for tonight, Mom had better find a hockey mask, because sleeping in the same bed with a four-year-old is a bruising experience.

EPILOGUE

Taking discipline action is easiest when a parent is wide awake and thinking clearly. But at 1:45 AM, most of us are pretty fuzzy. Here the temptation to yield is at its peak. So what does one do? Get out of bed, swat a bottom, walk a child to the corner, put him firmly back in bed? Perhaps, if one has such stamina and resolve even when half-asleep.

On the other hand, if sleep is a must, the discipline can be delayed. For example, in the morning when Wakefield seeks his first privilege, "Mommy, can I watch *Fun-time at Bedtime?*" Mom can respond, "Oh, not today, Wakefield. You didn't stay in bed last night. You need to stay in your bed to get TV." For each additional perk, Mom can answer in kind, "Oh, not today, Wakefield. You didn't stay in bed last night." Her aim is to teach Wakefield just how costly it is to make bedtime unpleasant, especially once she is in bed.

With the most stubborn preschoolers, this multi-consequence approach usually retires the problem in a week or less. And to answer the question, "What happens if Wakefield refuses the corner after leaving bed?" the same strategy will work: favorite privileges revoked the next day, with the number and kind at the parent's discretion, depending how exhausted she is.

Sometimes it is better to put off until tomorrow what you are too tired to do today or, more specifically, tonight.

CHAPTER 3

Champion Cliff Diver

Actors: Dad; Grandma; five-year-old Cliff; Grandpa (cameo appearance)
Scene: Grandma's living room
Time: Sunday afternoon

PROLOGUE

A grandparent who protects her grandchild from his parent's proper discipline not only undercuts the parent's discipline but also hurts the child she means to help.

Dad: Cliff, what did Grandma tell you? She said to quit climbing on the back of her couch. Now get down.
Grandma: He's OK. He's just being a little boy. You were a lot more rambunctious when you were his age.
Dr. Ray: Which is it? Does Grandma want Cliff off the couch as she asked? Or is he allowed to climb because Dad was once a little Cliff? Yes, Cliff may be "just being a little boy," but if being a little boy entails being disobedient, then it needs to be curtailed. Most childish misconduct, in fact, could fall under the umbrella of "just being a kid."

In short, Dad's level of childhood rambunctiousness is completely irrelevant to whether or not Cliff should be disciplined.
Grandma: He won't do it again, will you, Cliff?
Dad: Mom, he's already done it five times while we were sitting here. And you told him every time to get down. He needs to listen.

Grandma: I know, and he will. He's just full of energy.

Dr. Ray: As Bill Cosby has said, "These are not the same people who raised us. These are older people now trying to get into heaven."

It seems that even though Grandma wants Cliff to quit foot-mauling her furniture, she doesn't want anyone to go so far as to do something about it. She's waiting for Cliff to cooperate because she asked nicely. Yes, he is full of energy, but it's energy directed at ignoring her.

Dad: Mom, if you want him to stay off the back of the couch, I'll make it happen.

Grandma: Cliff, did you hear your dad? He wants you to stay off the back of the couch.

Dr. Ray: In the dialogue of good cop–bad cop, Grandma just can't bring herself to play the heavy. While Dad and Grandma continue to debate the likelihood of Cliff's cooperating, he takes advantage of the distraction, hoisting himself up for another leap.

Dad: That's it. Cliff, you go sit on Grandma's red chair. And don't get up until I tell you.

Grandma: Awww. He wasn't being bad. He's just having fun.

Dad: Mom, he disobeyed you and me, more than once.

Grandma: He just got carried away a little, didn't you, Cliff? Come over here and sit on Grandma's lap.

Dad: Mom, he needs to learn we mean what we say. I told him to sit. Now, Cliff, get on the chair.

Grandma: OK, I'll sit over there with you, Cliff. We'll sit together, OK?

Dr. Ray: When a relative wishes to nullify a parent's discipline, she often directs her comments toward the child. Grandma likely thinks Dad is being "too strict." In fact, just the opposite is true, as Cliff was warned five times about being a couch diver. Hardly a premature jump toward discipline on Dad's part.

Dad: Cliff, I said you need to sit by yourself for not listening to me or Grandma.

Cliff: I'm sorry, Grandma. I won't do it again.

Dr. Ray: This child is a quick study. He senses he has a much better chance of dodging the chair if he keeps the conversation between him and Grandma, leaving Dad to talk to himself. Cliff realizes, at least for the moment, where to throw his allegiance. Grandma is obviously on his side, so he'll solidify the partnership a little more.

"I'm sorry" is good, but it doesn't free one from the results of one's conduct. Try telling an employer, "I'm sorry," after showing up late five days in a row. See if he or she says, "Oh, that's OK. You're just being an employee."

Cliff is now safely ensconced in Grandma's arms, looking at Dad as if to say, "I'm sitting, OK?"

Grandma: See, he just needed a little time to settle down. He'll listen next time, won't you, Cliff?

Dad: Mom, he needs to listen to me this time.

Dr. Ray: Grandma, whether meaning to or not, has effectively thrown Dad under the bus or, if you will, under the couch. She's sent the message to Cliff that as long as she's around, he has an ally, and that it's acceptable to question Dad.

Grandpa (walking in): Well, isn't this nice? Cliff is sitting on Grandma's lap. You really love your Grandma, don't you, Buddy?

Cliff: Uh-huh.

EPILOGUE

In fairness to grandparents everywhere, I hear just as often from the older generation that they wish their kids would better discipline the grandkids. They'd like to enjoy some laid-back grandparenting, but they feel they can't, as that would just exacerbate the lax parenting.

Dad has two basic options. Option one: He can pry Cliff from Grandma's arms and enforce his discipline. Probably, though, that would create a scene nobody wants. And what about the next visit, and the one after that?

Option two: Dad might say something like, "Mom, he needs to learn to listen to me and to you too. If you don't let me discipline him here, I'll have to do it at home. And he'll be in even bigger trouble. So you'll just make it worse for Cliff by covering for him."

Dad could also tell Cliff prior to each visit to Grandma's house, "Cliff, if I tell you to do something at Grandma's, you'd better listen. If you don't, when we get home, you'll go straight to the corner."

Cliff has shown himself to be a fast learner. It shouldn't take too many visits before he realizes that, no matter how much Grandma buffers him from Dad at her place, he does have to go home. And Grandma won't be there to protect him. Unless she follows him home. Which I'm not sure I'd put past her.

CHAPTER 4

Up for the Count

Actors: Dad; six-year-old Tarry
Scene: The swing set in their backyard
Time: Near dinnertime

PROLOGUE

Preschoolers count to show how smart they are. Grown-ups who count when disciplining preschoolers aren't being too smart.

Dad (from the patio door): OK, Tarry, time to stop. Dinner's on the table. Let's go; I already gave you ten extra minutes.

Tarry: Just ten more swings, then I'll jump off. One, two, two...

Dad: No, no more swings. It's time to eat.

Tarry: Two, three...

Dad: Tarry, stop counting and come in now. One... two...

Dr. Ray: Tarry is not about to immediately change pursuits at Dad's initial say-so. Between food and fun, most little kids lean toward the latter. (That priority tends to shift the farther one journeys into adulthood: another example of life's being wired backward.)

Apparently, prior to today Dad has counted on his numbers to get compliance. Otherwise, Tarry would have little idea what the counting means. A count only motivates if in the past it has signaled a raising of the discipline stakes.

Tarry (not jumping off, but no longer kicking his feet, not literally anyway): OK, I'm almost done.

Dad: No, you're not almost done. You are done. Get off the swing, now!

Dr. Ray: Tarry is offering his notion of a compromise, thus convincing Dad, "I'm in the process of compliance." As is routine in the numbers dialogue, Tarry is not responding with alacrity. He is, if you will, dragging his feet. What dilatory tactics the typical child presents is bounded only by his creativity and his parent's patience.

Dad: You can slow down quicker than that. Do you want me to start counting again?

Tarry: I'm slowing down as fast as I can. These swings are big, and I'm little.

Dr. Ray: Dad is putting his discipline in question, as in, "Do you want me to start counting again?" As I recall, he didn't finish his first count. Nevertheless he resumes the count, backing up two numbers and upping the volume.

Dad: ONE... TWO...

Tarry: OK, OK, I'm coming. I have to slow down more so I can jump off without hurting myself.

Dr. Ray: This kid's good. He's painting a picture of cooperation even as he's not cooperating. Had Dad continued the count he started back when, he'd probably be somewhere around sixty-seven, sixty-eight....

Let's take a second swing at getting more timely cooperation.

Dad: Tarry, you have ten seconds to stop swinging and get to the house. If you don't, you don't go back out tonight. (Whereupon Dad silently begins to count. Or like a basketball referee, he displays with his fingers how the time is ticking.)

Tarry (taking three of those seconds to gauge whether or not Dad plans to say anything more): OK, OK, I'm hurrying.

Dr. Ray: There is an irony to counts. It seems they send a louder message when silent. Call it the uncertainty factor.

For Tarry, Dad's new tack has an upside and a downside. The upside is that he gets ten seconds instead of three. The downside is that, within those ten seconds, he has to abandon the swinging life, make it to the patio door, open it, and step inside—though while in motion he still has time to form his argument about what exactly Dad means by "get to the house." To the patio? To the step? To the door itself? Tarry may come to regret the day he asked Dad to set up the swing set at the far end of the yard.

EPILOGUE

Counting carries a number of drawbacks.

One, counts are seductive. Initially they may persuade a child, mostly through his fear of the unknown. That is, he is unsure what lies beyond the final toll. With repetition, however, counts can teach delayed obedience. "I'll wait to see if or when Mom is going to move, and only then will I slowly move." In a child's mind, "When you start to count, I'll start to listen."

Two, the count can evolve into the discipline itself. The numbers come to substitute for real consequences. Many's the mom or dad who, upon arriving at the final number, is lost as to what to do next. Having linked their authority to the numbers, they are left adrift discipline-wise when the count reaches its terminus.

Three, counts convey an unspoken message: I really don't expect you to listen to me when I first speak. I'm satisfied if you eventually come around. Put another way, I'm giving you a window within which to consider my request. If that's what you mean to convey, count away. If not, why invite the delay, with all its potential for friction?

In the end, whether the count is to three or thirty-three, Tarry will probably meander ever so slowly toward the house, thereby seeming obedient—in his own time.

CHAPTER 5

Know Your Audience

Actors: Mom; Dad; seven-year-old Oscar; five-year-old Emmy
Scene: The family SUV; kitchen; bedroom doorway
Time: 7:45 PM, after a cousin's birthday party.

PROLOGUE

Parents who argue over discipline within kid earshot don't typically settle on one winner and one loser. All too often nobody wins, young or old.

Mom: What you did at my sister's was embarrassing, and I think the kids felt it too.
Dad: I don't see anything I did as embarrassing to anybody. If anything, the kids were embarrassing me by acting so wild while Moore was opening his mountain of gifts.
Mom: That's just the point. It was dragging on, but they were just being kids. OK, they got a little excited, but you can't expect them to sit on their hands for forty-five minutes.
Dad: A little excited? Is that what you call Oscar's jumping up and grabbing the block set from his cousin?
Mom: He gave it right back. Besides, Emmy didn't do anything like that. Why did you make her put her head down at the table too? Every other kid there was cranked up. Why did you single ours out and make them look bad?
Dad: I'm not the father of every other kid there. If I were, they wouldn't be allowed to act so obnoxious. Our kids are our

responsibility, and if they're out of control, I have to do something about it. Your sister could benefit from reading a couple of Ray Guarendi's books on discipline.

Mom: She doesn't even like his stuff.

Dr. Ray: Maybe she'd listen to a CD.

Normally, about four minutes into the thirty-one-minute ride home from Auntie's, both kids are dozing off in the back seat. Not this ride. Too much is happening in the front seat. The kids are staying wide awake for the duration.

Mom: I can see why you might send Oscar out of the room, but Emmy? She was behaving all right.

Dad: That's true, if you call "all right" running in circles around the room and diving into the nearest lap every time Moore opened a new present. There must have been twenty of them.

Mom: My sister feels guilty about Moore's father leaving them, and she tries to compensate.

Dad: Well, maybe she'll see how our kids get disciplined, and she'll realize that her kid needs it too.

Dr. Ray: If Mom and Dad were home, this debate could be conducted someplace out of the kids' earshot (on the roof?). As it is, the kids are four feet away, twelve miles from their beds. Every article of disagreement is of interest to juvenile ears, and that's in nobody's interest. Mom is upset, and Dad is defensive. Not a good formula for settling disputes.

The time is ripe for Oscar to weigh in. His words are addressed to Dad but meant for Mom.

Oscar: I didn't like being the only one to miss Moore's presents. I was at the table a long time.

Dad: No, you weren't. You were there for about fifteen minutes.

Mom: That's a lot for a child his age. The experts say one minute per year of age in time-out.

Dad: Which "experts"? They can't agree among themselves, and they aren't raising Oscar; we are.

Dr. Ray: The notion lurking beneath this mom-dad disagreement is a common one: "psychological correctness." That is, there are correct and enlightened ways to raise children, as espoused by some expert or experts. With this in mind, one parent disagrees with the other because his approach is judged to be insensitive, strict, or too controlling—just downright in error.

Unlike some experts, reality is more broad-minded. It recognizes a wide range of psychologically correct correction. What one parent sees as wrong often is merely a variation from her method or style. Therefore, as a rule, one parent's questioning the other in front of the kids causes more problems than the "problem discipline."

Time for child number two to cast her vote for the preferred parent, at least for tonight.

Emmy: I was crying at the table. Everybody thought I was bad.

Mom: Nobody thought you were bad, Sweetheart. (To Dad): See, in front of everybody, they both were embarrassed. Couldn't you have waited until later—after the party, or at least after the presents? It seems like our kids are always the only ones getting disciplined.

Dad: That's because nobody else there disciplines their kids when they should. At least ours know what we expect. I'm not going to change what I do because of what somebody thinks.

Dr. Ray: It sounds as though Mom may be as anxious over "looking bad" as she is over Dad's party parenting. Still, a protracted "who's right" conflict is begging the kids to choose sides. And they naturally will. Guess whose?

Oscar: When I got off the table, I went to play with Moore, but he was already playing with Conan, and they didn't let me play.

Dr. Ray (Translation): See, Mom, what Dad did. You're right. Keep up the pressure!

Emmy (Quietly crying).

Mom: You won't have to deal with them tonight. I will. I'll be the one who puts them to bed, and I'll have to settle all of this down.

Oscar (arriving at home): Mom, do we have to go to bed yet? I'm not tired at all.

Emmy: Yeah, can we stay up with you?

Mom: OK, maybe a little, if you hurry up and get your jammies on.

Dr. Ray: The youngest of kids have a honed sense of timing. The key to a successful request is the *when*. And Mom is primed to provide a bedtime counterbalance to Dad's earlier "mean" discipline. Note the "Can we stay up with *you?*"

Dad: They know which side their bread is buttered on. They heard every word of what we were saying, and who do you think the good guy is in their eyes?

Mom: They were half-asleep. They'll forget all this by tomorrow. I still think you overreacted. They need discipline, but not then and there. Sometimes you just have to let stuff go.

Dr. Ray: Mom is right—sort of. Yes, the kids likely will forget the particulars of this debate. No, they aren't likely to forget the theme. Mom and Dad aren't on the same discipline page. And they can make book on that.

Dad (entering the house behind Mom and the kids, talking to her back): When I think they need discipline, I'm going to discipline, no matter where we are and no matter who's watching.

Mom: You can discipline, but you didn't need to get so loud. The way you raised your voice, you made a scene.

Dad: What scene? All I did was remove them, and most of your relatives probably agreed with me. Somebody had to be a parent in there, and the kids were a lot quieter after that.

Dr. Ray: Mom tarries in the kitchen for several minutes and then heads down the hall, only to find both kids still in party clothes, standing just inside their bedroom doorways. If they had pencil and paper, they probably would be taking notes on their parents' discourse.

Oscar: Mommy, can you come in my bedroom with me? (Mom enters.) Dad was really mean at the party. I didn't have much fun after that. I just wanted to go home.

Emmy (Coming out of her room, hugging her mom's leg, saying nothing but being extra-clingy).

Dr. Ray: Mom may be convinced that the kids were temporarily "traumatized" by Dad's display of authority. Likely not so. What is so is that the kids read their parents' script, assessed which parent is their ally, and are aligning themselves with her, leaving Dad back at the party by himself.

Mom had best be careful. In the future, if she's seen as the bad guy, and Dad "protects" the kids from her, she too could be isolated. Kid alliances can shift as rapidly as the discipline wind.

EPILOGUE

Discipline disagreements are stoked and sustained by some common templates: I'm right—you're wrong; the experts agree with me—not you; you're too hard—you're too soft; you over-reacted—you ignored.

Few would argue about the value of parents' agreeing on discipline. And rightly so. But agreeing is best interpreted to mean "agreeing on standards," not necessarily on how to teach and enforce those standards.

No two spouses agree everywhere and always on discipline—not as long as each is an individual. No two personalities, histories, tolerance levels, and voice volumes are exactly alike. Thus a parent regularly practices the details of discipline his or her way. The goal is to not be too far from one another or, when so, to disagree agreeably. Otherwise other family members, a.k.a. children, will be quick to locate the cracks (fissures?) in the parental wall.

Most parents are not extreme in their discipline. That is, it would fall within a range considered appropriate or "healthy." Do they differ in consistency? Probably. Do they differ in strictness? Possibly. Do they sometimes dislike the way the other handles or doesn't handle some piece of misconduct? Yep. All that is normal and to be expected. The trouble arises from arguing over legitimate differences and trying to correct the "wrong" parent in full eye- and earshot of those "wronged."

As a child, I learned my parents' discipline speed limits early. My mother's was 35 m.p.h. My father's was 20. I adjusted my speed accordingly. Though my mom at times allowed us to exceed her limit before ticketing us, something told me she liked having my dad's limit being that of a school zone.

CHAPTER 6

A Blackout With Power

Actors: Mom; eight-year-old Buck; five-year-old Will
Scene: Kitchen; kitchen corners
Time: Midmorning

PROLOGUE

The main discipline question for many parents is not what consequences to levy when. It is how to enforce those consequences when a youngster opposes them.

Will (bursting into the kitchen, drama-crying, hand covering his forehead): Mom, Buck punched me in the head, really hard, and it hurts.

Buck (eight feet and two seconds behind Buck): No, sir. He came over and grabbed the car I had on my track, and he wouldn't give it back. So I had to grab him and make him give it back. You always say I need to stick up for myself.

Dr. Ray: From Kid Manual, section 107-B: I'm only doing what you've told me to do—at least as I interpret it.

Mom at the moment has no foolproof means of scratching out the truth. Still, she is not without evidence: The red mark on Will's forehead is a near perfect match with the middle knuckle on Buck's right hand.

Mom: Buck, did you hit him?

Will: Yeah, he did. Look, right here on my head. See, and it hurts bad too.

Dr. Ray: From Kid Manual, section 205-C: Don't risk letting your brother answer; preempt it. Simultaneously reemphasize that "it hurts bad too," just in case Mom didn't catch the first complaint.

Buck: He grabbed my car, right off the track, and then he started laughing. I told him, "That's not funny."

Dr. Ray: These boys have memorized the whole manual. Hear how Buck did not answer his mother, instead redirecting the focus of the fracas back to Will. The child has a future in politics, or possibly psychology.

Will: I didn't take your car. It was just sitting on the floor. You weren't even playing with it. (Punctuating his point, Will kicks his brother's leg.)

Mom: That's it. Both of you to the corner. Buck, you're by the refrigerator. Will, you go over by the clock. I need to think about what else I'm going to do about this.

Dr. Ray: Corners are prime discipline real estate for kids, especially the younger ones. First, they are ubiquitous. The average room has four of them. For those of you with larger families, should you fill up one room, you've got others.

Second, they are dull. With one's face pressed between two walls, boredom is an unavoidable byproduct.

Third, they are multipurpose. They can be called upon for a range of offenses, at a moment's notice, repeatedly if necessary.

Mom's corner reliance has a twofold purpose—as discipline and as a pause for her to ponder added consequences. She apparently believes that assaulting a sibling is an impactful offense that warrants more than a few minutes in time-out. (In our home, hitting a sibling brings on automatic loss of all privileges.)

Buck (from the corner): I'm always the one who has to go to the corner because you believe Will all the time. I wish Grandma was my mom; she never puts me in a corner. I wish Dad were my mom; he understands boys.

Will (crumbling to the floor, launching into a tantrum, once again holding his head): I didn't do anything. He started it. Why do I have to go to the corner?

Mom: Will, you need to get to that corner immediately. Buck may have started it, but I saw you kick him. And Buck, your time doesn't start until you're quiet. And the longer either of you carries on, the longer I make your time even after you're quiet.

Will (both hands on his forehead, running from the room): No, no, no!

Dr. Ray: Mom is trying to reason past the trouble, but reasoning with an irate five-year-old (indeed, any age kid) is like trying to persuade a mother grizzly to leave her cubs in your care.

What now? While Buck has quieted—mostly to let Will be the sole focus of Mom's discipline attention—Will has exited, stage right. Mom could pursue, but if she meets more resistance, the scene could get really ugly. And even if she can make Will comply, she could lose some authority.

A simple rule of discipline: If you have to fight with a child to enforce your discipline, you may win, but he also wins by challenging your authority. Mom can show more calm, resolute authority by implementing what one of my clients called "blackout." Let's illustrate.

Will (six minutes post-defiance, figuring Mom has forgotten the corner): Can I have some juice, Mommy, in my dinosaur cup?

Mom: Oh, no, Will. You can have some milk, but not in your dinosaur cup. You have to go to the corner first.

Will (in stunned disbelief, melting down again): My head hurts. I want my stuffed dog.

Mom: Your stuffed dog is on top of the refrigerator. You can't have any toys until after you go to the corner.

Will (eight minutes later, after quieting once more, still in shock over what's happening): Can I watch *The Dino Show*?

Mom: I'm sorry. You can't watch anything until I get all your corner time.

Dr. Ray: And so it goes. All perks, privileges, and goodies are suspended until Will serves his corner time. A preschooler or young child typically needs only a few episodes of blackout to realize how definitely a parent means what she says. He will learn fast that it is far better to take her discipline—whatever that may be—than to be blacked out.

The average teen does take longer to accept blackout conditions, but most are back to civilization by their wedding rehearsal dinners.

Will (one hour, twelve minutes later): OK, Mommy, I'm going to the corner. How long do I have to stay?

Mom: I'll let you know when your time's up. But because you didn't go when I said, your time is longer now.

Dr. Ray: Wait just a time-out minute! Don't experts intone: "One minute in time-out per year of age"?

Some do, mostly the ones without kids. But you, not they, are the parent in your home. You set the time, depending upon factors like immediate cooperation, the quickness to quiet, and the seriousness of the infraction. Mom may believe that Will's face and Buck's leg (both got hit) are worth more than eight and five minutes in the corner.

By the way, where's Buck? No doubt, he is taking a positive view of this new thing called blackout—at least until it happens to him. Let's rewind an hour or so.

Buck: I love you, Mom. When I come out, I'm going to give you a big hug and kiss. And then we can pray together too, OK?

Dr. Ray: So smooth. If at first vinegar doesn't succeed, try honey. And for good measure, make sure you contrast your holiness with your brother's sinfulness.

Is Mom fooled?

Mom (sometime later): OK, Buck, you can come out now, and we will pray. But after that I want you to sit down and write fifteen nice things about your brother.

Dr. Ray: I'll bet that's not what Buck was praying for.

Will: Buck, you better do what she says.

EPILOGUE

Blackout—some parents call it "shutdown"— is powerful discipline. It makes a clear statement: Please do not defy my discipline, or I'm prepared to act very firmly.

All kids misbehave—lots. But when they challenge your authority—passively or actively—they have escalated dramatically from "routine" misbehavior to direct defiance. And if you lose the authority to enforce consequences, well, how much rent will you pay your kids to live in their home?

While adolescents may endure it longer, in some ways blackout carries even more leverage with them. Teens have a much broader array of activities, privileges, and "entitlements": transportation, technology (cell phone, computer, iPod, video games, television, headsets), favorite clothes, eating out, curling iron, money supply (funds are frozen, meaning school lunch is packed). The list is extensive, and only you know what would constitute a full blackout in your home, as opposed to a brownout.

Some parents also use blackout for serious offenses—time is either automatic or linked to improved attitude and cooperation. Sometimes my wife blacks herself out. Retreating to her bedroom, she locks the door and naps. I stand outside the door, begging her to share her blackout with me.

CHAPTER 7

Wake Up Call...and Call...and Call

Actors: Mom; nine-year-old Rip

Scene: Rip's bedroom; the bathroom; the stairs; the kitchen

Time: Monday morning and afternoon

PROLOGUE

It isn't so much school that kids resist. It's that they have to wake up to go there.

Mom (6:55 AM, from the bottom of the stairwell): Rip, let's go. Didn't you hear your alarm go off again? I could hear it from down here. You've only got twenty minutes before the bus gets here.

Rip (Barely audible): Yeah, OK.

Mom (7:00 AM, louder, and two steps up the stairwell): Rip! Get up now! You won't have time to even eat anything. We're not going to go through this every morning.

Dr. Ray: When a parent proclaims, "We're not going to go through this every (fill in the blank)," she is saying one of two things. One, we have in fact been going through this for some time. And two, this is not the first time I've said, "We're not going to go through this."

In her second attempt to rouse Rip, Mom illuminated a core discipline equation: $C=1/(N+V+D)$. Translation: The degree of cooperation (C) is inversely proportional to the number of naggings (N) plus the volume (V) plus the distance (D). In plain English, the more and louder a parent talks from a distance, the less likely she is to get cooperation.

From her first to second wake-up call, Mom did move closer to Rip by two steps, thus decreasing D, but two steps aren't enough to shift the equation much in her favor.

Rip: I'm getting up.

Mom: You'd better be. I'm not going to take you to school again because you missed the bus.

Dr. Ray: Meaning: I have before and I probably will again, but I'm not telling you that. Rip is doing his imitation of a snooze alarm. Every five minutes he buzzes something about getting out of bed and then heads back to his pillow, hoping for a few more reprieves before Mom travels all the way upstairs.

Mom (7:05 AM, heading into Rip's bedroom and shaking him awake): That's it. You're going to get an earlier bedtime from now on. If you're this tired every morning, you're not getting enough sleep. I said, "Get up." I mean it. Now!

Dr. Ray: Mom may not realize it, but with her bedtime threat, she stumbled upon a fitting discipline, which we will detail right after school.

Mom's surging frustration is evidenced by her addendums: *I mean it* and *now*. Do they mean she didn't mean it ten minutes ago?

Rip (sitting on the edge of his bed): OK, OK. I'm getting up. Can I have some toast?

Mom: I don't know if you'll have time for anything now. Hurry up and get ready, and maybe I can get you something to eat before the bus gets here. You should have thought about breakfast while you were lying in bed.

Dr. Ray: With Mom heading for the kitchen, Rip starts to dress with the speed of a snail on crutches.

Mom (7:10 AM, from the kitchen): Rip, where are you? Your toast is ready. You'll have to eat it at the bus stop. Come down before it gets cold.

Rip (muffled): I'm going to the bathroom.

Mom (racing upstairs, seeing Rip's socks and shoes still on the bedroom floor, and rapid-fire knocking on the bathroom door): What?! You're not even dressed yet? What have you been doing?

Rip: I had to go real bad. I'm almost done.

Dr. Ray: For kids, few rooms in the house provide better sanctuary from discipline than the bathroom. Parents, too, especially those of young children, regard the bathroom as a retreat center.

The tension is growing. The bus's appearance is looming; Rip is still in slow motion; and Mom is feeling the futility of trying to move him forward. All the ingredients for nonstop friction are in place.

Mom: If you don't come out now, you won't make the bus. You know it sometimes comes early, and if you make me take you to school again…

Dr. Ray: "If you make me take you to school again," then what? Mom is on the verge of using an effective "if-then" discipline statement, that is, "If you do X, I will do Y." However, she is leaving off the Y, the most crucial part of her statement. Perhaps she is unsure exactly what will constitute her Y. Or she's hoping that the vague threat of some kind of action will motivate Rip.

"Ifs" without "thens" can initially succeed, mostly through a youngster's fear of the unknown. With repetition, though, they go unheeded, as they evolve into another variant of nagging.

At 7:17 AM the bus's beckoning honk resonates through the front door. Not only is Rip's footwear still two rooms from his feet, but he's just now emerging from his bathroom cocoon. At 7:18, as Rip nearly trips down the stairs, the bus pulls away. More evidence that his tardiness has been his pattern, as the driver's tolerance for delay is much shorter now than in September.

Mom: Great. You missed the bus again. I ought to let you just miss school unexcused and tell them to do what they need to do. This is getting ridiculous. You're nine years old, and you can't get yourself ready for school. And I'm not going to dress you.

Rip: I'll get my stuff.

Dr. Ray: Dressing Rip, as we shall shortly see, may in fact be Mom's best discipline option.

Mom: Grab your toast and get in the car. This is the last time I'm going to do this. Now I have to wake up your little sister and take her with us.

Dr. Ray: My guess is that with all of the morning fracas, little sister is probably wide awake already.

In insisting, "This is the last time I'm going to do this," a parent would do well to think about what she will do next time, in case "this" isn't the last time. For now Mom seems not to have thought about next time. If she had a discipline plan, and conveyed it clearly to Rip, she would lower the chances there would be a next time.

Something tells me the ride to school isn't going to be too pleasant, for Mom or Rip. Hopefully they'll make all the lights.

EPILOGUE

Most misconduct or noncooperation is recurrent. Is this because children are incorrigible creatures who repel guidance and instruction? Not really, most of the time anyway. It is because they are children, period. And as savvy child psychologists, they will persevere with behavior that works for them, until a parent perseveres longer with discipline that works for her.

Obviously the morning melees have been ongoing. Witness Mom's surplus agitation and the bus driver's limited patience. The connection is predictable: The more unyielding the timeline, the more parental pressure to induce a child's cooperation. And the more adept a child can become at maneuvering around that pressure.

Nonetheless, parents have options. Immediate discipline is not always necessary. Sometimes the misconduct can be allowed to run its course, to be dealt with at a more opportune time. Let's apply this principle to Mom and Rip, as we fast forward to 3:10 PM.

Rip has just bounced in the door, having jauntily put the morning tug-of-war into his sleepy past.

Mom: Rip, I'm sorry we had such a bad morning. I don't like starting off your school day like that. So I'm not going to nag you to get ready anymore. When I hear your alarm, I'm going to come up, wake you, and if I have to, help you get dressed. Then I'll supervise your tooth brushing and escort you down to breakfast.
Rip (Smiles, as if to say, "I was wondering when you'd see it my way.")
Mom: But on any morning that I have to do any of that, I'm going to figure you are too tired to get ready yourself and that you're just not getting enough sleep. So that night you will go to bed one, maybe two hours earlier, depending upon how you cooperated.

Rip (A look of stunned disbelief seems to say, "Wait a minute. I thought we had already laid out our morning ritual. I was at peace with it; I was one with the morning.")

Mom: One more thing. If I ever have to drive you to school again, however long it takes me is how much work time you will owe me first thing after you get home.

Rip (Gags in disbelief, as if to say, "Who are you? Where is my mother? Are you an alien in her body? Were you reading one of Dr. Ray's discipline books again?")

Dr. Ray: Older kids can be charged mileage for any of Mom's bussing made necessary by irresponsibility, noncooperation, or social sabotage.

Mom has not only pulled free from Rip's molasses morning; she is schooling Rip: I will hold you accountable for making me cooperate with your noncooperation.

The "discipline delay" principle isn't limited to school mornings. It can fit any scenario constricted by whatever factors: a time crunch, a public place, a critical relative, a potential "scene." Like a skilled bullfighter, a skilled parent knows when to flow—for the moment—with charging trouble. "Later" will offer a much wider array of consequences, along with time to sort through the best ones.

One mom told me she didn't want to wait until later. Upon hearing her son's alarm, she quietly climbed the stairs armed with a spray bottle of water. The early morning facial mist usually sufficed to rouse her slumbering son.

My wife had only one question: Would that work on husbands?

CHAPTER 8

Someone to Watch Over Me

Actors: Mom; her mother; nine-year-old Gideon
Scene: On the phone; Gideon's bedroom
Time: Monday morning, October 16; Saturday night, October 21

PROLOGUE

A well-behaved child doesn't behave well only for some adults and not others. He behaves well for all, even weak disciplinarians. If not, his parents must discipline for them.

Grandma: Jade, is something bothering you? You seem a little down this morning.

Mom: I got another call from Gideon's religion teacher last night. This is the third one. She says that he's disrupting the class and that he's not getting any better for her. Actually, he's gotten worse, she says. Now she wants me to come into class and sit with him.

Grandma: Is she a good teacher?

Mom: That's just it; she's not. The few times I've looked into the room when I've dropped Gideon off, it was chaos. He can't be the only one in there who's giving her trouble. You'd think they'd at least get somebody who can control a bunch of third-graders.

Dr. Ray: Whether there's another disruptive child in class, or three, or ten is beside the point. Mom's responsibility is Gideon. It's clear Mom has little confidence in the teacher. It's real clear she thinks that were the teacher a better disciplinarian, her son would be a better student. It's really, really clear that she is not keen on the idea of sitting in class and monitoring Gideon. She's already passed third grade.

Grandma: Can you call her and see if there isn't something else you can do? I mean, how can she expect you to go in there every week? There are some people who just shouldn't try to teach.

Mom: I asked her that last night. She's said she's had other parents do this before. Apparently this isn't the first time she couldn't handle a nine-year-old. Then she implied that if Gideon doesn't settle down, they might have to remove him from class.

Dr. Ray: Grandma means to be supportive, but she is fueling Mom's denial. Maybe the teacher is as weak as Mom thinks; maybe she isn't. That's hard to know. What is known is that Gideon is being quite uncooperative. And that is the core issue, not the teacher's child-management skills.

Let's assume that the adult "at fault" for being unable to corral a rambunctious child can set in motion a downward spiral. Is this the only adult, or are there others? Will the child push ever harder, thereby requiring ever more competent adults to control him? Weak or strong, no other grown-up is my child's primary disciplinarian. I am.

Grandma: Do you want me to go in and sit with him? I've got more time than you do.

Mom: No, that's OK. This isn't your problem. Besides, if Gideon sees Grandma in class, he'll just think it's more fun time. Maybe I can get Skip [his father] to sit in there a few times. But that'll be a struggle. He misses church half the time.

Dr. Ray: Reading between the lines (I can do that since I'm writing the lines), Mom is admitting that Gideon isn't all that well-behaved for Grandma either. The spiral is spinning: Gideon sounds inclined to resist any grown-up he sees as his unequal. Mom too?

Mom: I know he can be a handful. He's tough for me, but last year's teacher didn't have any problems with him. She never once complained about him.

Dr. Ray: Once more, beside the point. This year's teacher does have a problem with him. What's more, we can safely assume that Gideon is older than he was a year ago. The natural course of misbehavior is to get more frequent and intense if allowed. Last year's teacher, too, might have trouble with Gideon if she had him this year.

Grandma: Why don't you talk with his teacher one more time? I'll go with you if you want. We can ask her if there's some other way to help her with Gideon.

Mom: I guess I could try that. But if we can't come up with something, maybe I'll just have to pull him out and hope he gets a better teacher next year.

Dr. Ray: Short of squeezing into a third-grade desk, Mom has other options, as we shall hear shortly. Perhaps she hasn't tapped into it yet, but she has plenty of authority to compensate for what the teacher lacks, even if she's six miles from that classroom.

The gospel truth must first be accepted: Gideon is giving his teacher (a volunteer, no less) a bad time. True, if the teacher were stronger, if she had a 6-foot-6, 280-pound assistant, or if she had a trained sheepdog, Gideon might be more cooperative. But she isn't and she doesn't. Nor should she have to.

Grandma: What if you just went in a few times? That might be enough to settle him down.

Mom: I really don't want to embarrass him. It'll look as if his mommy has to come with him and sit by him. I don't think he'd like that at all.

Dr. Ray: What Gideon likes is not relevant here. Embarrassment isn't always bad. Sometimes it's just the push (fear?) a child needs to behave well on his own.

EPILOGUE

The ultimate goal: A youngster who acts well with everyone, not just with the competent, the "liked," or the six-foot-six. So someday, as an adult, he will continue to act well with everyone, not just the authoritative—a police officer, a judge, a wife.

Mom is being called to act in place of Gideon's teacher. Obviously, if the teacher were more effective—as Mom sees it, that is—Mom wouldn't need to do anything. Since that is not the reality, Mom must do something to hold Gideon accountable for mistreating his teacher.

So what can Mom do? She's not taking third-grade religion again. Well, she could; she's been invited. Whether Gideon is mortified or not, he will see up close and personal where Mom sits regarding good behavior. And only a few visits might suffice to clear his vision.

Or it might take no visits. One mom of a class-cutup ninth-grader gave him one week to shape up, or she would be his new classmate. She meant it; he knew it; she never had to do it.

If Mom can't do the in-class thing, she has alternatives. Let's jump ahead to the next Saturday night, as Mom informs Gideon of her new classroom rule. Any new rule is made more memorable, especially with younger kids, when presented as close to the troublesome scenario as possible. Mom could wait until Sunday morning in church to unveil it, but that probably would be disruptive, not to mention irreverent.

Mom: Gideon, your religion teacher tells me that you haven't been behaving for her in class.

Gideon: I don't like her. She has her pets, and she's always telling me that I'm not acting right.

Dr. Ray: It seems Gideon has sensed Mom's lack of confidence in his teacher. And he's ready to agree wholeheartedly.

Mom: None of that matters here. Your dad and I expect you to behave for her. So here's what we're going to do: One of us will check with your teacher after every class to see how you did. If she says you gave her problems, all the rest of the day you will have no privileges at all. You will also go to bed early, and you will write her a hundred-word apology. If she says you were fine, you will have all your privileges.

Gideon: But she's not a very good teacher.

Mom: But you have to be a good student. If we get a bad report a second time, you will have two days without privileges. And you don't want a bad report seven or eight times. That's a lot of days without privileges.

Dr. Ray: Good conduct for all—teachers, grandparents, neighbors, coaches—unquestionably has to be enforced by one—the parent. When our children misbehave for us, we still love them. Most others do not have our emotional connection. For them to like our child, he must be likeable. That's where we act if necessary.

CHAPTER 9

Swinging Siblings

Actors: Ten-year-old Victor; eight-year-old Wiley; Mom; Mrs. Cravatz, the neighbor lady
Scene: Backyard swing set; patio; patio door
Time: Any afternoon with swing-set weather

PROLOGUE

It's not all that hard to unravel a sibling squabble. All you need are whole-house security monitors, a judge and jury, one nosy neighbor, and paid informants. Then you'll have a fifty-fifty chance.

Victor: Come on, Wiley. You've been on the good swing forever. This other one doesn't go as high for somebody that's bigger.

Wiley: You had your time this morning. Now it's my turn.

Victor (moving menacingly toward Wiley): You've had a lot of time. You've been on it a lot longer than I was. Now get off.

Wiley (defiantly kicking his legs to take the swing higher and faster): No way, Victor. You'll just have to wait until I'm done.

Victor (grabbing at the swing, slowing its trajectory and bringing it to a stop): Oh, yeah? We'll see.

Wiley (kicking at Victor): Quit it! You don't own this swing. Leave me alone!

Victor (grabbing Wiley's leg, pulling him off the swing onto his backside): Yeah, I'll leave you alone, after you get off.

Wiley: I'm telling Mom, Victor. You're gonna be in big trouble.

Dr. Ray: Sibling quibbling needs only seconds to escalate into an all-out dogfight.

Now, unless Mom is riding the swing next to Wiley, she will be pretty much blind as to who swung first in this oscillating altercation. Though we know that a higher percentage of blame is Victor's, Mom doesn't. She may suspect so, but she has no incontrovertible evidence. What's more, after refereeing countless clashes, she may be close to defeat, in part from repeated, unsuccessful efforts to sort out who did what to whom, when and where, and in part from accusations by both parties of blind injustice.

Mom: Look, you two. I don't know what's going on out there, but work it out. I'm not going to get in the middle of it.

Wiley (running back toward his swing, now occupied by Victor): Mom says to give me the swing. You already had it enough. She wants me on it now.

Dr. Ray: Wiley, figuring his brother is out of Mom's voice range, tries to spin this into his victory. The real winner, though, is Victor. Whether from fatigue or from reading one too many parenting articles, Mom is falling back on one of the more unrealistic, not to mention awful, child-rearing dictums: Let siblings solve their own disagreements. Allow them the chance to develop their skills of conflict resolution. (The conflict almost always rules over the resolution.) Don't get involved unless someone is getting hurt. (What kind of "hurt"?)

If I were Victor, I'd be scattering issues of *Modern Sibling Today* all over the house. This "work it out yourselves" approach is perfect for me. I'm the older brother. I'm bigger, stronger, probably smarter, and overall more dominant. Even if Wiley is weaselier,

hen two or more kids are involved, and you can't figure
exactly with whom more blame lies, the course most "fair"
ough the kids won't agree) is to discipline all.

hildren can work it out themselves as long as they meet several
ditions: no physical contact (other than hugs and kisses), no
me-calling (other than first names), no nastiness of any kind. If
one of the conditions is broken, refer to principles 1 and 2.

here is only one foolproof way to reduce sibling quibbling to
o: Allow only one child at a time to live in your home. Or at
very least, keep them on different floors, separated by fences
moats guarded by trolls.

most of the time I still win.

I wouldn't be inclined to propose, "OK, Wiley, since I'm older, it's up to me to take the lead in settling our disagreements. After all, I remember what it was like to be eight years old. So let's set up a win-win. You swing first until you're tired. I'll push you if you need help. Then I'll swing longer later. See? Problem solved."

Let's return to Planet Earth.

Wiley: Mom says you have to let me swing as long as I want, 'cause you had it first this morning.

Victor: No, she didn't. I heard her. She said for us to figure it out ourselves. And we already did.

Wiley (charging the swing): Victor, you're a jerk. You always have to have everything your way. I'm gonna get in your way until you get off.

Victor (pumping his legs faster): Go ahead. See what happens.

Wiley (knocked down by Victor's flailing feet, runs toward the patio door): Mom, Victor kicked me on purpose, and it really hurts.

Dr. Ray: So much for a mutually acceptable solution. And what can we really expect? At ages ten and eight, the boys are incompletely socialized, partially self-controlled, morally immature human beings. This description is not harsh. It is reality. And that's why 78.26 percent of the time (my informal assessment), having siblings "work it out themselves" doesn't work. It assumes way too much about childish nature that isn't true. Furthermore, becoming a teen and thus presumably more adultlike doesn't necessarily foster improved negotiating skills either; it may actually constrict them.

Mom (at the door): Now what's going on? I told you two to figure it out. Now you've made me have to get involved.

Mrs. Cravatz (walking through the yard toward Mom): Hi, Susan. I saw what happened. Both boys had a role in it, but it looked as if Victor started it. You know, Susan, I've noticed some things about the boys...

Dr. Ray: And this is why the brothers, particularly Victor, are not all that fond of Mrs. Cravatz. Nevertheless, if Mom can't afford a security camera...

Mom: Victor, you get off the swing now and give it to Wiley. Wiley, you've got twenty minutes, and then it's Victor's. I don't want to have to come out here again.

Victor (jumping off the swing in a huff, casting a quick glare at Mrs. Cravatz and a longer "I'll deal with you later" one at Wiley): Fine, I don't need to swing at all. You always believe what Wiley says.

Wiley: Hi, Mrs. Cravatz. How are you?

Dr. Ray: It seems this time, Wiley likes how it all worked out.

EPILOGUE

Sibling quibbling is high-frequency misconduct, which defies unraveling much of the time. As such, it can prompt befuddlement, inconsistency, and exhaustion. If a misbehavior occurs ten to twenty times a day—not an uncommon total for only two siblings, a low total for more—a parent will struggle to reach even 20 percent consistency.

So it is with the boys' mother. While she does offer a compromise for the impasse, she does no actual disciplining. Neither son feels any consequences for provoking the other, even when it went physical.

What then could Mom have done? Let's rewri[te] her script some new lines. Any one is best del[ivered] first hit the door and before Victor first hit Wil[ey].

Mom: OK, all swinging is over. In the house, b[oth] for the day.

or

Mom: Wiley, you get the first half hour; Vict[or] hear any more bickering, there will be no half [hour]

or

Mom: Come on in, boys, and sit at the kitchen [table until] you're ready to cooperate.

or

Mom: Hey, guys, any more trouble, and you'[ll] for an hour.

or

Mom (getting creative): OK, inside, boys. Yo[u] table and write fifteen nice things about your b[rother].

or

Mom (getting crazy creative): Each of you wil[l] the swing for fifteen minutes, singing, "He a[in't heavy, he's my] brother."

Dr. Ray: To tone down sibling quibbling, h[ere are some] principles:

Zero tolerance for mistreatment of a sib[ling]. squabbling is "normal"; that doesn't mean it [is] something for all family members. And that [is] not just voiced.

"Action" discipline not only reduces sibling [conflict]. discipline. Rule: Consistent discipline leads to [nothing] more.

most of the time I still win.

I wouldn't be inclined to propose, "OK, Wiley, since I'm older, it's up to me to take the lead in settling our disagreements. After all, I remember what it was like to be eight years old. So let's set up a win-win. You swing first until you're tired. I'll push you if you need help. Then I'll swing longer later. See? Problem solved." Let's return to Planet Earth.

Wiley: Mom says you have to let me swing as long as I want, 'cause you had it first this morning.

Victor: No, she didn't. I heard her. She said for us to figure it out ourselves. And we already did.

Wiley (charging the swing): Victor, you're a jerk. You always have to have everything your way. I'm gonna get in your way until you get off.

Victor (pumping his legs faster): Go ahead. See what happens.

Wiley (knocked down by Victor's flailing feet, runs toward the patio door): Mom, Victor kicked me on purpose, and it really hurts.

Dr. Ray: So much for a mutually acceptable solution. And what can we really expect? At ages ten and eight, the boys are incompletely socialized, partially self-controlled, morally immature human beings. This description is not harsh. It is reality. And that's why 78.26 percent of the time (my informal assessment), having siblings "work it out themselves" doesn't work. It assumes way too much about childish nature that isn't true. Furthermore, becoming a teen and thus presumably more adultlike doesn't necessarily foster improved negotiating skills either; it may actually constrict them.

Mom (at the door): Now what's going on? I told you two to figure it out. Now you've made me have to get involved.

Mrs. Cravatz (walking through the yard toward Mom): Hi, Susan. I saw what happened. Both boys had a role in it, but it looked as if Victor started it. You know, Susan, I've noticed some things about the boys...

Dr. Ray: And this is why the brothers, particularly Victor, are not all that fond of Mrs. Cravatz. Nevertheless, if Mom can't afford a security camera...

Mom: Victor, you get off the swing now and give it to Wiley. Wiley, you've got twenty minutes, and then it's Victor's. I don't want to have to come out here again.

Victor (jumping off the swing in a huff, casting a quick glare at Mrs. Cravatz and a longer "I'll deal with you later" one at Wiley): Fine, I don't need to swing at all. You always believe what Wiley says.

Wiley: Hi, Mrs. Cravatz. How are you?

Dr. Ray: It seems this time, Wiley likes how it all worked out.

EPILOGUE

Sibling quibbling is high-frequency misconduct, which defies unraveling much of the time. As such, it can prompt befuddlement, inconsistency, and exhaustion. If a misbehavior occurs ten to twenty times a day—not an uncommon total for only two siblings, a low total for more—a parent will struggle to reach even 20 percent consistency.

So it is with the boys' mother. While she does offer a compromise for the impasse, she does no actual disciplining. Neither son feels any consequences for provoking the other, even when it went physical.

What then could Mom have done? Let's rewrite the scene, giving her script some new lines. Any one is best delivered after Wiley first hit the door and before Victor first hit Wiley.

Mom: OK, all swinging is over. In the house, both of you, maybe for the day.

or

Mom: Wiley, you get the first half hour; Victor, the second. If I hear any more bickering, there will be no half hours.

or

Mom: Come on in, boys, and sit at the kitchen table until I decide you're ready to cooperate.

or

Mom: Hey, guys, any more trouble, and you'll work in the yard for an hour.

or

Mom (getting creative): OK, inside, boys. You'll each sit at the table and write fifteen nice things about your brother.

or

Mom (getting crazy creative): Each of you will push the other on the swing for fifteen minutes, singing, "He ain't heavy; he's my brother."

Dr. Ray: To tone down sibling quibbling, here are some basic principles:

Zero tolerance for mistreatment of a sibling. True, sibling squabbling is "normal"; that doesn't mean it's good. Respect is something for all family members. And that has to be enforced, not just voiced.

"Action" discipline not only reduces sibling quibbling; it reduces discipline. Rule: Consistent discipline leads to less discipline, not more.

When two or more kids are involved, and you can't figure out exactly with whom more blame lies, the course most "fair" (though the kids won't agree) is to discipline all.

Children can work it out themselves as long as they meet several conditions: no physical contact (other than hugs and kisses), no name-calling (other than first names), no nastiness of any kind. If any one of the conditions is broken, refer to principles 1 and 2.

There is only one foolproof way to reduce sibling quibbling to zero: Allow only one child at a time to live in your home. Or at the very least, keep them on different floors, separated by fences and moats guarded by trolls.

CHAPTER 10

Driving the Discourse
One Way

Actors: Mom; ten-year-old Mario
Scene: Department store
Time: Any

PROLOGUE

In a child's mind, a parent is being most reasonable when she comes around to the child's way of thinking. And making a parent agreeable might take time, effort, and lots of words. But to the child it's well worth it.

Mario: Look, Mom. Mom, look. Here's that video game I was telling you about. The one I keep seeing on TV. It's really neat, and you said I could get it.

Mom: No, I never said you could get it. I said, "We'll see."

Dr. Ray: In parent talk, "We'll see" doesn't mean "Yes." It means, "I'm putting off my decision." In kid talk, "We'll see" signals that a "Yes" is only a matter of time and, if need be, some well-targeted nagging.

Unless one really does mean "Yes," it's smart to avoid the phrase "We'll see." It just asks for a protracted pushing for permission.

Mom: You've got plenty of video games. Grandma just bought you two more for your birthday. Besides, I don't know anything about this game.

WINNING THE DISCIPLINE DEBATES

Mario: Yes, you do. I told you before. It's the one where you have to drive a car through all kinds of traffic jams and see how fast you can get someplace. It's really cool.

Mom: It doesn't sound so cool to me. It sounds like it teaches you to be reckless. Anyway, forget it for this time around.

Dr. Ray: "This time around"? Is this a variant of "We'll see"? Is Mom unwittingly asking for more badgering next time around? And the next? In an effort to close the exchange for now, she's leaving it open down the road.

Mario: Mom, the ones that Grandma got me are for little kids. All they do is show you how to do some math facts that I already know.

Mom: That's good. It won't hurt you to get more practice. You don't know your math facts as much as you think.

Mario: Aw, come on, Mom. Just this one game. Then I won't ask for any more for a long time.

Dr. Ray: The next step after an appeal to a parent's "reason" has failed is an appeal to emotions. If that lands on a stony heart, execute the fatigue factor. Wear the big person down.

Mario: Mom, I already played it once at Chevy's house. His dad even played it with us. Please, Mom. It's my favorite of all the games. Please, huh?

Mom: No, Mario. Now, that's it. I'm not going to argue about this any more.

Mario: Mom, look. See, it says, "For ages eight and up." I'm ten. It's even got three stars on it because *School Mountain* says it's a good one for coordination.

Dr. Ray: Mom may be ready to quit arguing, but Mario isn't. He's keeping his foot to the accelerator. She'll have to be the one to slam on the brakes.

As an aside, notice the shaping power of "You've got to have this" advertising aimed at kids, even within the more "educational" television shows. The only way to limit its power is to limit its presence. Slow down on the TV. Mario won't be so acutely aware of the latest must-have goodie. And he won't be so driven to have it.

Mom: You can keep nagging all you want, Mario, but it's not going to work. I am not buying "Car Maniac" for you.

Dr. Ray: As the hectoring continues, Mom strives to stay resolute in the face of increasing words and volume. Not to mention the looks of nearby shoppers, especially ones with no children in tow. Sometimes offering an adolescent forty dollars per hour plus benefits to babysit while you shop alone is a small price to pay.

Mario: If I can't have it this time, maybe next time? When we get home I'll show you what games we can get rid of because I don't play them anymore. We can give them to kids who don't have any. I'll give away five for this one, OK?

Mom: We'll see.

EPILOGUE

It's a common script. Call it the illusion of resolve. A parent resists yielding to childish demands, even as they become more fevered. Standing her ground to the end, she feels the victor. But how much haranguing did she have to endure for how long? Further, was a pattern reinforced? That is, you can push on me, and I will tolerate it until one of us gets mad or exhausted.

You don't need to be a shrink to guess who will get to their limit first.

What if early in her "I don't think so," Mom would have sealed her decision with, "Mario, you got my answer. Please don't ask me again, or when we get home, I will take your favorite game, 'Atom Splitting Made Simple,' and keep it for a week."

Her message would be, "This exchange is really, truly over. If you don't park it now, there will be a fine, not to me but to you." And there will be no "We'll see" about that.

CHAPTER 11

I'm Honest, Honest

Actors: Dad; eleven-year old-Truman; eight-year-old Polly
Scene: Truman's bedroom
Time: Bedtime

PROLOGUE

Kids can bend, fold, and mutilate the truth with limitless creativity, particularly when the truth is to their definite disadvantage.

Truman (as Dad enters his bedroom): Hi, Dad. I'm just getting ready for bed. I'm pretty tired. I'll be asleep pretty quick.

Dr. Ray: Most kids instinctively sense when something unpleasant is brewing. Maybe it's seeing the wrinkle of a parent's brow. Maybe it's hearing the unusually heavy sound of a father's footsteps on the stairs. Maybe it's their own nagging guilt. Whatever, Truman is acting extra chirpy, a signal he's trying to set a sunny tone.

Dad: Truman, I was just downstairs in the family room. Somebody broke the lamp and tried to put the top back together but didn't do a very good job. Do you know anything about that?

Truman: No, I wasn't even in the family room tonight. Wasn't that lamp always kind of broke?

Dad: No. I used it this afternoon, and it was fine. You sure you don't know anything about this? Somebody was in there.

Truman: It might have been Polly. She was in there for a while. Maybe she knows how it happened.

Polly (lingering in the hall, waiting to report in): I was never in there; you were. I saw you. You were playing basketball with the pillows and the couch, and I heard you hit the lamp.

Dr. Ray: Now we have a sibling "he said–she said," one of the most perplexing of discipline scenarios. Does Dad full well know the particulars, or is he fishing for facts?

Dad: Truman, I don't need Polly to tell me what happened. I saw it for myself.

Truman (stunned as to how Dad is so sure): OK, I might have gone in there for a little bit, but I don't know how the lamp got busted.

Polly: Yes, you do. I heard you say, "Oh, great."

Truman: What are you talking about? I never said anything like that. You weren't even around.

Dr. Ray: If Truman is going to entangle Polly within his shifting story, she is going to bury him deeper. In response, he has to bury himself deeper into his fabrication. In case you're not sure, Truman is lying. I am sure, because I'm the author of this vignette. Polly is sure too, but because she has earned the reputation, rightly so, of being a habitual tattler, she cannot always be relied upon to give a complete and accurate report.

Hear, too, how Truman has just contradicted himself, all within one minute. First he says that Polly might know something, as "she was in there." Then he defends himself with "You weren't even around." Oh, what a web we weave....

Given Dad's line of questioning, he appears to realize, with or without Polly's witness, that Truman is not being forthright. The question is: When will he come forth with his judgment? He is trying, ever so gradually, to get Truman to admit to his infraction, with little success. Truman's operating template is: Admit to nothing until presented with a full-color, large-screen, real-time DVD recording. And even then he can claim it's been Photoshopped—by Polly.

Truman: Dad, honest, I don't know how it happened. Like I said, I think it was already broken.

Dr. Ray: It's an irony of childish denial that "Honest," when attached to an account, is often one sign that the account is anything but.

Dad: I know you broke the lamp, Truman. I not only heard you in there, but I saw you with the pillows when I was outside working in the flower beds. Now, do you want to tell me the truth?

Truman (Silence).

Dr. Ray: When busted beyond question, a youngster's default position routinely is silence. Cease any further verbal denial. Admit to nothing more. Hope the heat subsides for lack of fuel.

Dad: Truman, I'm a lot more upset about your lying than I am about the broken lamp. The lamp was probably just your being careless. Your lie is deliberate. I'm not sure what to do about this yet. For now, you are grounded to the house.

Polly: See, Truman, I told you. If you just tell the truth, you get in a lot less trouble. I know I'm the little sister, but...

Dad: OK, Polly, leave him alone, and come downstairs with me.

Dr. Ray: When facing a stiff-lipped youngster, Dad did what many of us parents are disposed to do: Haul out the bright lights and probe for an admission of guilt, or at least an acknowledgement of truth. And Dad met what many parents meet: a child doggedly determined to offer as little information as possible until it's clear the facts can't be massaged anymore.

Sometimes parents will try what I call the "inch by inch to the truth" approach. Here's how it would sound:

Dad: Truman, were you in the family room today?

Truman: A little.

Dad: Was the lamp on the table when you walked in there?

Truman: Uh-huh.

Dad: Is the lamp now broken?

Truman: I guess.

Dad: Are the pillows usually on the couch?

Truman: Uh-huh.

Dad: Is one of them on the floor next to the lamp table?

Truman: If you say so.

Dad: What happened?

Truman: I don't know.

Dr. Ray: Let's rewind to Dad's entrance into the bedroom and try a different tack.

Dad: Truman, I was just downstairs in the family room. The lamp is broken at the top. I saw you in there playing pillow basketball, and I know you broke the lamp. Now, do you want to tell me what happened?

Truman: Well, I did hit it...once, but I don't think it was hard enough to break it. It could've already been that way.

Dr. Ray: Truman is hanging by his nails. He seems convinced that's better than letting go. Notice too how he admits to Dad's facts without coming to Dad's conclusion. It's said that a rodent can squeeze through an opening that looks too small to accommodate his body. Kids squeezing through verbal cracks can make rodents look like amateurs.

When you know what happened, don't give a child a chance to be deceptive. Confront him with the facts, and if you wish, ask for details. It short-circuits a protracted "Did you? No, I didn't" interchange. Still, it doesn't always guarantee an instant admission.

Dad can try a further line of parenting:

Dad: Truman, I know what the truth is. I saw you knock over the lamp. So I'm only going to ask you once: Did you break the lamp? If you tell me the truth, you will have to pay for the lamp by losing your allowance for three weeks. If you lie, you will lose three weeks of allowance, get extra chores, write a five-hundred-word essay on the value of honesty, and be grounded for three days. Now, think carefully before you answer, because I'm going to accept whatever answer you give me.

Dr. Ray: No matter how defined the choices, some kids will still cling to their innocence. Call it a stubborn habit. Call it a belief that a parent won't follow through. Call it "plant whatever seeds of doubt I can." Who always knows the mind of a child, completely anyway?

Whatever Truman's answer, Dad is teaching a truth: The consequences of lying will always be significantly heavier than those for telling the truth. It may simply take multiple experiences for a child to believe this and choose honesty.

EPILOGUE

Why do some kids lie? Even when caught, and even when confronted with stiff consequences? For the most part, the reasons are not all that complex. There is no underlying psychological trouble. Nor is there an inability to separate fact from fiction. Nor does it predict a life of manipulation.

For most kids, twisting or flat-out denying the truth arises from one simple motive: Avoid trouble. Their strategy? Plant doubt. Admit to nothing, or to little when no escape route is possible.

Is this because by nature children can't be trusted? Is this because they have some hidden hostility to Mom and Dad's rules? Not typically. It is because their consciences are not yet strong enough to overpower their innate urge to dodge discipline. And that is why they need parents to teach them—over and over—the inestimable value of truth-telling.

Truth be told, a skillful lie is hard to catch. Kids can get away with it. So, no matter how consistently a parent disciplines discovered deception, some deception just goes undetected. A lying habit can be exasperatingly durable. That doesn't mean it can't be broken. It means it may take longer to do so than a parent thinks.

However stubborn any misbehavior, parental perseverance is the key to breaking its grip. Honest. Would I lie to you?

CHAPTER 12

He Said; She Said; Mom Said

Actors: Mom; eleven-year-old Nat; nine-year-old Tattalia

Scene: Any place beyond Mom's eyeshot but within her earshot

Time: Thirty-six seconds after siblings began occupying the same room

PROLOGUE

Children with siblings have well-formed consciences. They know exactly what is right or wrong—for a brother or sister.

Tattalia (loud enough for Mom to hear): Nat, quit it. Get away from me. You know you're not supposed to do that. Mom won't like it.

Nat: I'm not doing anything. Stop trying to get me in trouble.

Dr. Ray: Like Mom, I can't really see what's happening in there. All I hear is a disagreeable dialogue between two parties who for the moment are looking at life quite differently. I would strongly suspect, however, that both voices are strategically aimed in Mom's direction, to inform her of who is doing what to whom. In fact, I doubt the kids are talking to one another as much as they are talking to Mom.

Mom: What's going on in there? Do I have to come in?

Tattalia: He won't leave me alone. I'm trying to work my puzzle, and he keeps pointing where to put the pieces.

Mom: Nat, is that true?

Nat: No, I was just trying to show her how to put the hard pieces where they belong. I didn't even touch them.

Dr. Ray: Nat is not about to admit, "Why, yes, Mother, it is true. I am irritating my sister by my mere presence. Thank you for pointing this out."

Nat sees himself as offering brotherly guidance. Tattalia sees him as provocative. And Mom hasn't seen anything yet. This puzzle is going to get more intricate before it gets solved.

Mom (still in the other room): OK, Nat, just let her put her own puzzle together. Tattalia, he was only trying to help you; you don't need to get that upset.

Dr. Ray: For a brief instant, Mom is satisfied that she has found, if not a resolution, a compromise. She's added a peace to the puzzle.

Tattalia: Mo-o-o-o-m! He's looking right at my puzzle on purpose. He thinks I'm not doing it right, I can tell. Make him sto-o-o-o-p.

Dr. Ray: One value of vowels is that they allow kids to linguistically draw out a whine. A professional tattler can prolong an *a, e, i, o,* or *u* to emphasize her point. Hear, too, Tattalia's shift from Nat's overt misconduct—pointing—to his covert misconduct—looking. In essence, "I'm going to tell on you for even thinking about bothering me."

Tattalia (sensing Mom is not about to directly intervene, abandons her puzzle and seeks her out): I'm just trying to do something by myself, and he keeps on bugging me. I don't know why you let him do that.

Dr. Ray: If Mom won't act on the basis of Tattalia's "facts," Tattalia will question Mom's sloppy parenting, implying that inaction means injustice. Without realizing it, Tattalia has just tattled on herself. She's shown that her motive for involving Mom is not to work her puzzle uncoached but to make certain that Nat receives a good piece of discipline.

Mom: Nat, get in here. Let her work her puzzle. You two can't even be in the same room without somebody complaining.

Nat: She's always trying to get me in trouble. And you believe her. You didn't even see what happened. Why do you always believe her first?

Dr. Ray: Nat is taking a page from Tattalia's playbook: When arguing one's case, make sure to throw into question a parent's style or fairness. Mom is now being accused from both sides. Either she isn't defending the "victim," or she's prejudiced in the accuser's favor. What's a parent to do?

Mom (heading into the focus of the fracas): All right, that's it. Nat, you leave the room; Tattalia, you put the puzzle away. If you two can't even get along over something as simple as a puzzle, then I'll just separate you and take the puzzle.

Tattalia (crying as she leaves the room): All I was doing was playing by myself, and he wrecks it all every time.

Nat: I didn't wreck it. You did by running to Mom just because I don't act the way you want.

Mom: I can't let you two out of my sight without problems. You both are puzzles to me.

Dr. Ray: Mom has reached her limit, which then prompts action. But when frustration propels discipline, it can lead to overreaction. Also, Mom is most moved to intervene after each child has attacked her discipline personally. Kids know what buttons to push, but sometimes it backfires on them.

EPILOGUE

What is the core issue here? Is it sibling quibbling, or is it tattling? Or some of both? Initially it sounded as though a typical brother-sister wrangle was brewing, but even when Nat appeared to buzz off, Tattalia pursued "justice" as she defined it.

The main plot seems to revolve around tattling. Some kinds of tattling are healthy. A parent does need to know when something serious or intervention-worthy is happening. And siblings, however idiosyncratic in their accounts, can be valuable sources of information, at least as starting points for excavating the truth.

In my experience, a really bad house rule is "No tattling allowed. All tattling will be ignored." This only gives kids full license to act with impunity whenever out of a parent's eye- or earshot, which is most of the time. Some tattling deserves to be heeded.

Then again, much tattling is born of ill intent. Its purpose is to retaliate against a sibling via the long arm of a parent's justice. "Nail him for what I just told you he did, said, or thought about doing to me."

In this scenario, Mom could have stepped sooner into the room—assuming she wasn't occupied or hiding somewhere, like the bathroom—and put an end to Tattalia's escalating accusations.

Mom: Tattalia, it sounds to me like you want him out of this room, no matter what he's doing. He is allowed to look at your puzzle. So if you tattle on him again, I won't discipline him, but I will put your puzzle away. You decide.

Dr. Ray: Mom's words could come as quite a shock to Tattalia, as in her mind, she's the faultless one. I mean, how can any reasonable person expect her to endure her brother's "looking"?

Is Nat totally innocent? Hardly. But while he did backtrack on his provocation, Tattalia didn't. She wanted, if not a pound of flesh, at least a few ounces.

Much of dealing fairly with a tattler's revelations is about reading intent. Unfortunately, reading intent is one of the tougher puzzles of parenting. It's one I've yet to find all the pieces for.

CHAPTER 13

For My Ears Only

Actors: Mom; twelve-year-old Earhard; five-year-old Andrew; Dr. Ray (age unknown)

Scene: In front of the television; Andrew's bedroom

Time: Two football game quarters and one halftime past Mom's request for help.

PROLOGUE

Discipline is action, not words. The more a parent talks, the less she is heard.

Mom (walking in and moving to turn off the TV, by hand, as Earhard has all four remotes): I see the only way I'm going to get you to clean up your mess is to make it happen. Your dishes from lunch are still on the counter, and I asked you three times now to take out the trash. Let's go.

Earhard: Mom, I told you I'd do it. Why does it have to be done right now? There are only two minutes left in the game, and then I'll get it.

Dr. Ray: Veteran parents, as well as savvy wives, know that in real time the final two minutes of a football game are about half the length of a geologic era. The issue is not Earhard's gaming of the clock but his obliviousness to Mom's multiplying requests.

Earhard did declare, "I told you I'd do it," which in kid-talk means, "As long as I have the intent to get to it eventually, don't bother me with it right now." Or, "I agreed to do it, so you should be happy. Don't ask me to actually do it."

Mom: Why is it, Earhard, that if I want you to do something for me, I have to wait until the time is just right for you?

Earhard: Mom, I said I'd do it. The game is almost over, and I watched it the whole time. This is the best part. It's only two more minutes.

Dr. Ray: Translation: "I can't believe you are being so impatient and unreasonable." Never mind that Mom began her appeals an hour and a half ago, during halftime. Earhard is playing upon her ignorance of football. Whereupon, not wanting to be the grinch who stole the game, Mom gives Earhard two more football minutes or two days, whichever comes first.

Mom (realizing that Earhard has gone beyond her two-minute warning, returns to the family room): Earhard, is that game over? What are you watching now? Football guys talking about the game? You said that when the game was over, you'd clean up your mess.

You know, Earhard, you don't realize how easy you've got it. When I was your age, I was already helping my mother every day around the house. Every Saturday morning we got up early and cleaned. I always made my bed and my little sister's too. We didn't have a dishwasher; I was the dishwasher. We were taught that the house was everybody's house.

We knew that you worked first, then played, not the other way around. And the TV never went on until we were done with our work. That's just the way it was. I did what I was asked because I was asked, not because I was told ten times. And you know something else, we were grateful for what little we had, and happy. You seem to think...

Dr. Ray: I don't know where Earhard is sitting right now, but I would guess that even though he's likely less than six feet from Mom, he doesn't see or hear her.

Mom has turned to a staple of parenting: the lecture. Lectures are animated by the yearning to be understood. If we just talk/explain/enlighten until we're close to passing out, if we just contrast our childhood with theirs, if we just chronicle the mature kid we were, some bit of something will penetrate, and a flickering emotional light will brighten. After all our effort we will be rewarded with gratitude for our soul-shaping monologue. If only it were so easy.

Earhard: I know, Mom. You were a great kid. Just ask Grandma.

Dr. Ray: Earhard is more responsive than most, as he did utter a few sentences, however patronizing. Most kids just stare (into the floor or space), grunt a few barely audible syllables, or begin a rhythmic series of eye rolls, head droops, sighs, and "whatevers." Children—until they themselves are parents—are convinced that our childhood has no relevance whatsoever to theirs. Sure, we may have walked to school barefoot in a foot of nuclear waste, but that's only because the earth was still cooling, and our moms were afraid the heat would ruin the one pair of shoes we had for six children.

For her part, Mom is convinced that if her first couple of thousand words don't register, add more.

Mom: I was your age once, you know, and I knew that if I was going to get any privileges, I had to be responsible. I was the oldest, just as you are, and my parents expected a lot out of me. For the life of me, I don't understand why you drag your feet so much. Life is not all play. You're at the age when you should be doing a lot more around here. When I was six, I did more than you do now.

Are you even listening to a word I'm saying? I'm not talking just to hear myself talk, Earhard. Earhard?

EPILOGUE

Lectures aren't always for our ears only. They can actually edify a juvenile, provided (1) children, including adolescents, are eminently reasonable creatures, (2) children see parenting through the eyes of a parent, (3) children are eager and grateful to hear about their misconduct, (4) children like being corrected (Don't all humans?).

If your youngster fits two or more of the above, by all means, lecture away. But the faultier these assumptions, the more likely it is that you'll go unheard, no matter how many words you pile up and for how long.

My oldest son, Andrew, taught me my first personal lesson about lectures when he was five years old. He had lied to his mother and was sent to his bed, and my wife wanted me to "talk" to him. As I am a highly trained professional communicator, this interchange would be child's play. Allow me to recount this memorable exchange.

Dad: Andrew, Mom tells me that you lied to her.

Andrew: I don't remember.

Dad: Andrew, if Mom says you lied, you lied. Now, I'm going to ask you again, and you'll be in more trouble if you lie to me too. So, did you lie?

Andrew: I still don't remember. But if Mom says I did, there's probably a pretty good chance I did.

Dr. Ray (commentary): What a squishy answer. This child needs a good talking to about honesty. And I'm just the one to do it.

Dad: Andrew, I want to talk to you, son.

Dr. Ray (commentary): I proceed to instruct him for several minutes about trust, about my own father's hurt the first time I lied to him, about the value of one's word, along with every other illustration I could muster for good measure. Our eyes were locked. Our hearts were one. I was on a fatherhood roll. God willing, one day thirty-plus years from now, Andrew would confess at our Thanksgiving table, "Dad, I never have thanked you for the talk we had when I was five—the one that permanently changed the course of my life."

As my final therapeutic flourish, I asked a therapeutically open-ended question.

Dad: Well, Andrew, do you have anything you'd like to say?

Andrew: Yeah, Dad. How come when my one eye looks at the ceiling, my other eye can't look at the floor?

Dr. Ray (commentary): Somewhere in my mini-speech I lost that boy. And I think it was when I began, "Andrew, I want to talk to you, son."

So am I advising, "Never lecture"? No. Lectures do have a place in parenthood. Certainly explain yourself fully when and where you judge best. And explore what's in your youngster's head and heart. But—and how many times am I going to have to tell you this—most lectures follow the law of diminishing returns: The more you talk, the less you're heard.

Let's rewind the tape and place Mom back in the TV room at halftime, the first time she spoke to Earhard.

Mom: Earhard, you've got all of halftime to clean up your stuff in the kitchen and take the trash out. If it's not done, you won't see the rest of the game. And you'll still have to clean.

Dr. Ray: Short, clear, to the point, consequential. But I just have to say one more thing...

CHAPTER 14

Car Repair

Actors: Dad; twelve-year-old Avis; ten-year-old Ford; seven-year-old Mercedes

Scene: The family minivan

Time: During the drive to a birthday party

PROLOGUE

Modern passenger vehicles are safer in many ways for children than those of the past. For one thing, they place kids further from a parent's discipline reach.

Avis: Scoot over. You don't need to hog the whole seat. Stay on your own side.

Ford: I am on my side. Why do you think the whole seat is yours? You get the best window every time.

Mercedes: Daddy, how come I never get to sit in the front? They always jump in first and push me out of the way.

Dad: Are you guys starting already? We haven't even gotten out of the drive yet, and you're at one another. You'd better settle down, or I'll turn this van around.

Dr. Ray: Car clashes don't always wait until the vehicle is in motion. Sometimes they begin with jostling for preferred seating— window, aisle, or first class. I'm seriously considering marketing a line of family-friendly vehicles equipped with spray-painted lines down the middle of the seats or, better yet, with dividing fences—electrified.

Until then Dad may have to levy some rules of the road. "I'm going to turn this car around" and my father's preferred "We'll just pull over and sit" are good options. The trouble is that something similar is threatened by parents about every 1.2 miles driven and actually enforced about every 23,612 miles. Not a good drive-to-park ratio.

Dad: Why do you guys start as soon as we get in the van? Why can't you just leave each other alone?

Ford: I didn't start anything. I was just getting in and sitting.

Avis: Oh, yeah. You were sitting all right—all over the whole seat. How much room do you need?

Mercedes: I didn't do anything, Daddy. I'm just sitting in my seat here in the back 'cause I never get the front.

Dr. Ray: The kids are not about to answer Dad's "Why do you guys start as soon as we get in the car?" so I'll answer it: for the same reason kids "start" lots of places—because they sense a parent's discipline options are limited, at least for the time.

When I was a child rider, my father could reach back and "correct" any one of us. For years I thought he had telescopic arms that could reach six or more feet. Nowadays, with the proliferation of vans, utility vehicles, and quasi-busses, kids might as well be sitting in the next area code for all an adult can do to intervene en route. Merely seated one row further back is comparable to being unreachably housed in an underground bunker two hundred feet below the surface.

Dad: If you don't settle now, when we get to the party, you'll all be sitting for a while.

Mercedes: Do I have to sit too? I didn't do anything. Those guys are the ones fighting, not me.

Ford: Oh, sure. You never do anything. Right.

Dad: I'm warning you. When we get to the party, you won't be part of it until I say.

Dr. Ray: Dad is realizing that even though this time around pulling over and sitting might be inconvenient or possibly unsafe, he isn't discipline paralyzed. He has options. Let's give him a few.

Dad: Every time I have to settle you down, that's ten minutes of sitting at Parker's party.

or

Dad: We can turn around and head back home; maybe we'll try later.

or

Dad: We'll pull into the next gas station, and I will listen to my music on the radio.

Dr. Ray: Dad is threatening psychological warfare. No telling how creative a parent can be when driven to his limit.

Mercedes, Ford, Avis (Stunned silence, with dirty looks being flung over and across the seats.)

Dad: Now, what station are those violins on?

EPILOGUE

Kids instinctively gauge what surroundings afford them a broad road on which to act with impunity—the car, church, a restaurant, Grandma's house, the psychologist's office. Nevertheless, a vehicle doesn't render children as out of reach of discipline as they assume. For one, often the family is headed somewhere the kids desire, allowing a parent to delay or cancel the destination in the event of car trouble.

Should the journey be toward somewhere less appealing—the store, Aunt Clara's house, the psychologist's office—discipline avenues are still open. There is no urgency to discipline *now*. There will be a time and a place soon, even if it's after returning home.

Not uncommonly my wife would pull into the garage, and at least three or four children would exit the van and head straight for kitchen corners. I could calculate the discord of any given trip by the number of corners needed. Two or less meant I was safe in asking, "How did your outing go, sweetheart?"

Perhaps the most effective discipline is the prolonged pull-over. Just one sitting has the potential to calm the next ten or so trips. Any time lost during a stop is well worth the peace and quiet gained on future rides. What's more, it only takes a couple of pull-overs to create the overriding specter of "She means it. She's done it before. One time we ran out of gas sitting in Wal-Mart's parking lot."

When our ten children were all under age twelve, my wife had the body shop install a double-paned, screened window between the front seat and the rest of the van, along with her picture and a sign reading, "Your friendly and courteous driver is Mom. To register any complaints, please call 1-800-Dads car."

CHAPTER 15

Am I Clear Yet?

Actors: Mom; twelve-year-old Oral
Scene: The minivan
Time: After-school drive home

PROLOGUE

A youngster who wants a social perk or privilege real badly will negotiate for it real relentlessly. And she won't quit until the negotiation comes to an end—an end almost always needing to be set by the parent.

Oral: None of my friends can believe you won't let me have a cell phone yet. I'm the only one I know of who doesn't have one. I'm old enough to pay for it myself.

Mom: We have been over this a hundred times, Oral. You don't need one, you are not old enough for one, and your friends can believe anything they want.

Dr. Ray: Like nearly all dead-end discussions, this one has been dialed up repeatedly in the near past. Mom acknowledges this, it sounds, to remind Oral she's not about to change her call no matter how much static she hears. Undeterred, Oral reiterates to Mom just how radically disconnected she is from the parenting norm—this being the cardinal sin in an adolescent's rules for life. Still Mom keeps angling for a clear reception.

Mom: Your dad and I will decide when you are old enough, and your age is only one piece of that decision. Right now you are not even close, so this isn't something you need to get upset about.

Oral: How old do I have to be? I am getting older, you know. How will you decide when I'm old enough? I get good grades; I never get in trouble; I do what you tell me. You say I have to be responsible, but it doesn't matter.

Dr. Ray: With indisputable insight, Oral informs Mom that this is as old as she's ever been. The implication being: I'm getting nearer to the magic age, whatever that is, but you'll probably just keep changing it anyway.

Oral's prime accusation, however, one aimed at engendering Mom's guilt and sense of unfair play, is, "I'm a wonderful human being, and this is the thanks I get." Mom is, in fact, rattled a little by this one.

Mom: You're a good kid, and I'm proud of you in lots of ways. But just because you are doesn't mean you will earn privileges that you aren't ready for yet. Being mature for your age doesn't automatically get you each and every freedom you want.

Oral: So how will I get freedom? I'm doing everything I can, and still it's not good enough. You just change the rules whenever you want. It makes me not even want to try anymore.

Dr. Ray: A veiled psychological threat: "Keep up your end of the bargain (as I've defined it), Mom, or I'll drop my end." In other words, be careful, or you'll push me into a retreat from responsibility, the very quality you say you want.

Mom: Oral, we give you lots of privileges. And that's because you do show maturity beyond your years. If you weren't who you are, you wouldn't have the freedoms you do have. But that doesn't mean your friends can decide what is good for you. As far as I'm concerned, I don't think any of your friends should have cell phones either.

Oral: Oh, wow, Mom. I never thought of it that way before. If I would just be quiet a minute and listen, I'd hear how much sense you make. I guess that's why you're the parent, and I'm the child. It's the wisdom thing, isn't it?

Dr. Ray: I confess, Oral didn't say any of that. I did. At this point in the interchange, it would seem the odds of her saying something similarly agreeable would be slightly less than those of getting a strong cell phone signal on the moon. She might later begrudgingly acknowledge Mom's point—to herself, not Mom—but right now her feet are planted more deeply with each point-counterpoint.

Let's go back to letting Oral speak for herself.

Oral: Oh, so now my friends are the problem. I don't see how you can think that. They all get good grades, too, and they never get in any kind of trouble either. That's why their parents trust them.

Dr. Ray: So there, Mom. Heard enough? Had enough? No matter how logical, how articulate, how patient Mom's explanations, each only serves to multiply Oral's comebacks. Nothing is settled; agitation only builds.

So what can Mom say to make Oral understand? Not much, but she can end the escalation.

Mom: Oral, we're going nowhere with all this. No matter what I say, or what reasons I give you, you won't agree. So before we both get too mad, I'm not arguing any more about a cell phone.

Dr. Ray: To further tone down future discord, Mom could add a post-text, employing some of Oral's own reasoning. Teens hate that.

Mom: Oral, you are absolutely right. Maturity does bring more privileges. And one part of maturity is accepting your parents' rules that you don't like. So if you keep badgering me about a cell phone, you'll just be telling me you're not as mature about all this as you need to be. You'd be smart not to keep bringing this up, because the more you push, the more I will push back the cell phone age.

EPILOGUE

As critical as when, where, and how much to allow a teen access to a personal cell phone is, that is not the crux of this scenario. The crux is: How long does a parent entertain objections that resist being answered? Not only is this particular exchange going nowhere, except maybe downhill, but all those preceding it likely have met the same fate. How do I know? Because the debate is still raging.

The key questions are: Is Mom being "insensitive" by cutting off this discussion sooner than later? Is anything to be gained by rebutting each and every point of contention, especially since they've all been answered "a hundred times" prior? Can Mom legitimately be accused of "not listening" if she ceases to argue?

Because parents long to be understood, we are susceptible to a frustrating parenting practice: dead-end debating. Once it is obvious that any parent explanation only leads to five more child objections, it's time to close the explanations. Such is not narrow-minded or autocratic; it is wise. If like discussions on like subjects lead to like outcomes—more agitation, less resolution, and accusations of "You just don't understand me"—why prolong them? Since the child won't be first to disengage, as he has little to lose and all to gain, the parent must.

Assume, for argument's sake, that at debate #203, a youngster finally comes to accept 12 percent of a parent's rationale. What was the cost during debates 1 through 202? How much emotional exhaustion and conflict resulted? What's more, does the chance of eventual peace rise or fall with the proliferation of battles?

My call on this? How about, "I gave you my reasons. You don't like them. If we keep going, we'll probably both get more upset." Then excuse yourself, as you have another matter pressing. Your nine-year-old wants to hear again why he isn't allowed to spend the night at Rutgers's house, especially since Rutgers gets good grades and his mom really likes you.

CHAPTER 16

Holding Court

Actors: Mom; Dad; twelve-year-old Eve
Scene: Kitchen; family room
Time: Two hours before a friend's sleepover begins

PROLOGUE

A parent who rules in favor of a child in a discipline clash with the other parent may score with the child, for the moment, but may not do what's best for the child.

Mom: Eve, I've had some time to think about this, and I don't think it's a good idea. I don't know who all is going to be there, and Mrs. Givin seems like a nice enough lady, but I don't know her all that well. I guess you could say I've changed my mind.

Eve: Oh, just like that: "I've changed my mind." For no reason. You said yesterday I could go, and now you say I can't. Whatever you say is the way it is.

Dr. Ray: Eve doesn't realize it, but she's right. Whatever Mom says *is* the way it is, at least in decisions regarding Eve's welfare. It's a parenting law that remains in effect for nearly twenty years—sometimes longer: A parent has the right, indeed the duty, to change her mind when she's determined a better course.

It is patently unreasonable—except when reasoning with the mind of a child—to think that a quite fallible human being, one whose parenting involves normal trial and error, will not make shortsighted, uninformed, or downright bad decisions. And correcting them is not inconsistency; it is wisdom.

Mom: You'd better settle yourself down, young lady. Yes, I did change my mind. And yes, it is going to be the way I say it is. There is no reason for me to let you do something that I think is questionable. And that's my final say on this.

Eve: Oh, yeah. How come your final say isn't what you said before? Why is "no" always your final say? You don't even have any good reasons why I can't go. I already called Dawn and told her and her mom I'd be there. Now what do I tell them? I can't believe this. There is nothing wrong with a sleepover with my friends. Every single one of their parents doesn't see any problem. How can all those parents be wrong, and you be right?

Dr. Ray: Mom has already argued too long, but if she wants to make one last rebuttal to Eve's last retort, she could say, "Well, they are, and I am." Of course, with Eve already on emotional fire, Mom's response would be verbal kerosene. Still, it may be true.

Because this scenario is on paper, it is not possible to convey the full demeaning tone of Eve's words. Suffice it to say, they are dripping with disgust. While Mom is going verbal toe-to-toe with Eve, she is getting pulled down to her level, and we are not the only ones to notice.

Dad (rising from his recliner, entering the kitchen): Just what is going on in here? What are you two fighting about this time?

Eve: She's being ridiculous.

Mom (Silent glare at both Eve and Dad).

Dr. Ray: Definitely not a good entrance by Dad. First of all, obviously he heard "what is going on" in there. Probably a few of the neighbors did too. His question is not a question. It is really a statement: "You two are going at it again."

Second, Dad right off is sending a message Eve no doubt loves and Mom no doubt loathes: I'm here to figure out who's doing what and to straighten out both of you. Put another way, Dad is about to hold court and to judge where the proper percentages of blame lie. Mom obviously read his entrance as such, hence the glare.

Eve: She told me I could go to the sleepover, and then, after I called Dawn and she got real excited about it, Mom decides on her own to just say no.

Dr. Ray: Notice Eve's phrasing: "Mom decides *on her own*." In other words, it's a tattle: "See, Dad, she never consults you. She thinks she's the boss." Mom immediately feels cornered.

Dad: I heard both of you getting agitated. Eve, you be quiet for now. Constance, now, why can't she go to the party again?

Dr. Ray: Stop the tape! Dad is digging his rut deeper and deeper. First he barges in looking to correct both parties. Then he begins his "fact-finding" by questioning his wife, implying she needs to explain herself to him, in front of Eve, no less. No question, Eve likes how all this is unfolding so far.

What's more, Dad has shown little or no interest in addressing Eve's disrespect toward Mom. This won't evoke his wife's admiration and goodwill. Let's give him a chance to reenact his entrance.

Dad: Eve, I don't at all like what I'm hearing from you. This is your mother you are talking to. If she has decided the sleepover is not a good idea, she has her reasons. You just don't like them. So now, not only am I with Mom on this, but you are in your room for the rest of the night for your nasty tone and attitude. Good night.

Eve: Fine. You have to do what she says, or you get in trouble. I didn't even get a chance to say what I had to say, but it doesn't matter. You won't listen; you'll just side with her.

Dr. Ray: Eve had expected Dad to be her sleepover savior. Instead he partners with his wife, making him the new target for Eve's scorn. Does Dad notice?

Dad: Well, Eve, you've just added to your discipline. You now have a five-hundred-word apology to write to both me and your mother, and tomorrow you are grounded from all privileges.

Mom (watching Eve trudge up the stairs): Thank you. She pushes on me hard, and sometimes I get so frustrated, I start to argue and don't stop. She pulls me in.

Dad: From now on, when I hear it, I'll step in and deal with her. You shouldn't have to take her mouth. If she sees both of us side by side in a decision, she's got no way to drive a wedge. Come here. Are you OK?

Dr. Ray: Something tells me Mom is feeling real affectionate toward Dad right now.

EPILOGUE

The ideal is that spouses are on the same page—or at least the same chapter—in decisions and discipline. The reality is that no two spouses are alike—in temperament, style, wordiness, consistency, or tolerance level. The best parenting teams are complementary. One partner supplies what the other lacks.

Mom readily admits that Eve provokes her and that she is slow to realize it. Dad doesn't help the dynamic if he enters the scene intending to sort out where Mom is wrong and Eve is right.

Even if Mom's style is poor, even if she over-talks, even if she over-negotiates, one unalterable fact remains: She is Mom. As such she has the right to make and change decisions. Yes, her approach might need to be altered some, but her God-ordained role as a mother is fixed. A judge's authority is not founded upon his courtroom demeanor; it is there by statute.

What would Dad's aim be in interrogating Mom, putting her on the defensive in front of Eve? Would it be to second-guess Mom's decision? To play peacemaker? To imply that if only Eve were handled better, she would be more respectful?

Dad's second entrance was far superior. First, he showed unity with Mom. Maybe he did disagree with her "no sleepover" decision. Nevertheless, Eve was on an ugly roll that needed to be stopped and disciplined.

Second, he aided his wife. Mom obviously felt some relief in not having to endure Eve on her own. Even better, Dad didn't step in with an attitude of "I'll bail you out, since you are too inept to handle a twelve-year-old." By focusing immediately on Eve's conduct, he made a clear statement: I'm here to correct my child, not her mother.

Finally, though Eve won't agree—at least until she's a bit older, say, sixty-eight or so—Dad's presence benefited her too. It does Eve no good, socially and morally, to permit her to adopt a style of "If my mother frustrates me, I'll let her have it."

Whether he realized it or not, Dad protected his wife, his marriage, and his daughter. All in all, not a bad payoff for abandoning the recliner for a few minutes.

CHAPTER 17

Reversed on Appeal

Actors: Mom; Dad; thirteen-year-old Holmes
Scene: Garage; upstairs bathroom
Time: 7:30–7:35 PM

PROLOGUE

Grown-ups have their ideas about the benefits of two parents raising children. Ask the kids, and you could hear, "Because it gives us two chances to get the answer we want."

Holmes: Hey, Dad. How's it going? Are you getting it fixed?

Dad (looking up from working on a lawn tractor): Well, I don't know. If I can't get it running this time, I might look around for another one.

Holmes (watching silently for about one minute): Hey, Dad, do you mind if I go over to Wendell's to watch a movie tonight? It's an OK movie.

Dad (struggling with a stubborn bolt, looking down again): Did you ask your mom? What did she say?

Holmes: I didn't ask her yet. I wanted to check with you first.

Dr. Ray: Holmes has set in motion a number of basic appeal principles. One, preface the request with a little bit of pleasant small talk. Two, approach a parent who is preoccupied or distracted. Three, acknowledge the decision-making authority of that parent. One wonders, had Holmes sought out Mom before Dad, would he have begun with the same, "I wanted to ask you first."

Dad: What time is it now? About 7:30? That's a little late to be starting a movie on a school night, isn't it?

Holmes: All my homework is done, and the movie has to be back tomorrow, so Wendell's family has to watch it tonight. He has school tomorrow too.

Dr. Ray: Hmmm. Since Wendell lives two doors down from Holmes, he probably attends the same school. Holmes is not updating Dad on the local school schedule; he is doing some parent comparing: Wendell has school tomorrow too, but his parents value family time. They're flexible.

One wonders: If Wendell were seen working in the yard until 9:00 PM, would Holmes object, "They sure are keeping him up late for a school night"? It's all in the context.

Dad: I'm not too sure about this. I don't know anything about that movie. Check with your mom; see what she thinks.

Dr. Ray: It sounds as though Dad wants to hear Mom's opinion; he isn't automatically deferring to her. I don't think it sounds that way to Holmes.

Mom is in the upstairs bathroom, getting ready to meet her cousin for coffee at 8:00 PM. She, like Dad, is immersed in the task at hand and thus is less able to fully ponder Holmes's proposal.

What's more, two floors, five walls, and forty-four feet separate her from Dad. Appeals rely upon an inverse relationship: The farther removed two parents are from each other—in place and in time—the less likely either is to confirm exactly what the other said.

Holmes: Mom, Wendell asked if I could watch a movie tonight with his family. The DVD has to be back tomorrow, so tonight is their only chance to watch it. It's that cartoon one, *Savvy Kid*

Lawyers. There's nothing bad in it. I already asked Dad, and it's OK with him if it's OK with you.

Dr. Ray: Well, not exactly. But exact enough for now. When arguing on appeal, paraphrase the first parent's words in the most consenting tone. It mitigates objections.

As he did with Dad, Holmes makes sure to tell Mom the movie night is "with his family." It never hurts to present one's case in the backdrop of family togetherness.

Mom: What did your father say?

Holmes: He said to see what you think.

Dr. Ray: Again, sort of. He did say that, but he also said some other things, like, "I'm not too sure about this," and, "That's a little late for a school night, isn't it?" Any ultimately successful appeal is very slow to include evidence that would hurt the cause.

Mom: Are you sure he doesn't care?

Holmes: He didn't seem to. He didn't tell me no. He told me to ask you.

Dr. Ray: "Are you sure he doesn't care?" seems to indicate that Mom has heard Holmes's appeals before. Her query, however, may be more rhetorical than fact-finding. That is, she probably doesn't suspect he'll answer, "Well, he does seem to care, but I figured I'd try to wrangle a better answer out of you."

For his part, Dad's response was a little too fuzzy. He left it wide open to paraphrase: Dad says it's OK with him if it's OK with you.

Mom: What time would you be home?

Holmes: It's a short movie. I can be home by 9:00, maybe just a little bit later. That's not even past my bedtime. Besides, tomorrow's Friday, and I can sleep lots after tomorrow.

Dr. Ray: As Dad needed to be reminded that the neighbor boy attends the same school as Holmes, Mom needs to be reminded that tomorrow is Friday.

Mom: Oh, all right. But tell your dad what time you'll be home because I won't be here when you get back.

Holmes (halfway down the stairs): OK, Mom, thanks. (Heading into the garage, slowing down just enough to apprise Dad of the final verdict.) Mom said it was all right with her and just to tell you when I'll be home. It'll be around 9:00 or 9:30 or so.

Dad (still struggling with rusted bolts, not looking up): Owww! Stupid blade! Just don't be late.

Dr. Ray: The time estimate is creeping later with each negotiation. Observe too that Holmes is already three steps down the driveway. His objective? Once a decision comes down in your favor, clear the court.

Mom (entering the garage, heading for her car): Did Holmes leave already?

Dad: He shot out of here after he got your permission.

Mom: My permission? I only said yes because I thought you said yes.

Dad: I never said yes. I wasn't keen on the idea, but I told him to check with you. I guess he did, in his own way.

Mom: He did, all right. And he made it sound as if you already had decided and just wanted to confirm it with me.

Dad: Do you want me to call him back for tonight?

Mom: I suppose we can handle this tomorrow. He's getting real good at playing us off one another. From now on we're going to have to check firsthand what the other said. Holmes's translations are slanted heavily in his favor.

Dr. Ray: Exactly. And to be expected. A loose answer leaves much wiggle room on appeal. Without directly falsifying the record, a youngster can leave out key details that would otherwise render a verdict against him—if you ask me.

EPILOGUE

So how does a parent bar repeated appeals?

First, if a request is not something that needs a two-parent agreement, don't seek it. If your decision is definite, say so. Put another way, it's real hard to make an appeal if an appeal is not granted.

Second, realize that whenever you do grant an appeal, the process could be coopted. Not necessarily because a youngster plans deception, but more because the temptation to act in his self-interest is powerful. Therefore, inform any appellant that you will confirm exactly what the other parent said, whether you are the first asked or the second.

Let's go to the bathroom again.

Mom: What did your father say?

Holmes: He said to see what you think.

Mom: Is that all he said? I need to know exactly what he told you, and whatever you tell me, I'm going to check out for myself. Remember, lying is a big offense.

Holmes: Oh, never mind. I didn't want to see that movie all that much anyway. And like Dad said, it is a school night.

Dr. Ray: All right. Almost no kid would drop an appeal so quickly or cooperatively. But I figured that the thought might be creeping into Holmes's head, as long as Mom was going to be so inflexible about all this.

A closing argument: Even with the best safeguards in place, some youngsters will still test the system. It is said that bats are able to slip through openings that look way too small to accommodate their bodies. When it comes to words, kids make bats look clumsy. They can squeeze through the slimmest of verbal cracks.

Upon later review, if you find that an appeal was based upon false testimony, confer with your spouse—face-to-face—and determine the appropriate sentence. In Holmes's case, Mom and Dad could decide to suspend his visits with Wendell for a week or two. In addition, they could inform him of a new house rule: Any fudging of answers will result in definite consequences, not reversible on appeal.

In law the appeals process is designed to safeguard the rights of the accused. It is supposed to work toward accuracy in judgment. Kids are savvier than lawyers. They've figured out how to make the appeals process work against accuracy. Who needs law school?

CHAPTER 18

Why, Oh, Why?

Actors: Dad; thirteen-year-old Chip
Scene: Behind the house
Time: Saturday

PROLOGUE

Wanting to know why is a powerful human drive. Asking a child why, however, often leads to no answer. When seeking the roots of a misbehavior, whys aren't always wise.

Dad is mowing in the backyard close to the house. Above the air conditioner, visible but not easily so, he notices "Chip and Holly" scratched deeply into the vinyl siding. Upon closer inspection his irritation breaks into action.

Dad: Chip. Chip! Come out here.

Chip (from inside the home): What?

Dad: Never mind "what." Just get out here.

Dr. Ray: "What?" is a child's reflexive response to a parent calling his name. "What?" is his way of saying, "Give me sufficient reason before I rouse myself to comply," or, "You don't sound happy, so I first need to know what I'm walking into."

Either way, "What?" can be considered a form of passive resistance. It really says, "I'm not coming until you make your case."

Chip (meandering warily into the yard): What?

Dr. Ray: As if to say, "OK, I came. Now what?" Not a respectful entrance.

Dad: What? No, I'll ask, "What?" (Pointing to the carving): What is this?

Chip (Leaning closer as if seeing it for the first time. Turning back to Dad with a puzzled "Huh?" on his face.)

Dad: Well?

Chip: I didn't think it would stay like that. I thought it would wash away.

Dad: And who is Holly?

Chip: Just a girl at school. I don't even like her anymore.

Dr. Ray: I guess that makes the carving acceptable then, as its original meaning is gone. It's a protective move: The reason for what I did then isn't relevant now, and if I had it to do over again, I wouldn't do it. So I shouldn't be in trouble anymore.

Once the motive is past, no need for discipline to correct me.

Dad: Well, it's pretty clear what you did. But why did you do it? You know better.

Chip (Blank stare, as if to say, "Why are you asking me this? I'm only the carver.")

Dad: Chip, I'm asking you again, why did you do this to our house?

Chip: I don't know.

Dr. Ray: At least Dad was rewarded with an "I don't know." Many parents receive a listless shoulder shrug, signaling: What? Who? Where? Me? Kids don't need attorneys to advise them. Instinctively they realize when charges are pending, and they reach for the Fifth Amendment. Their defense? The less said, the less incrimination.

Dad: You don't know? Who knows? Holly?

Chip: I didn't think it was that bad. I thought it would just be like crayon marks.

Dr. Ray: Kids are not complex creatures. Most day-to-day misconduct, even the unexpected bizarre stunt, is untangled by a few straightforward motives: (1) I had an impulse, (2) the opportunity presented itself, (3) I thought I could get away with it.

Still, parents are driven for more. The explanation just can't be that simple. Thus, in frustration a parent will resort to playing multiple choice. He'll provide the answers. All the child has to do is pick one.

Dad: Were you trying to impress Holly? Did you think I wouldn't see it? Were you not thinking?

Chip (Dumbfounded look, as if to say, "I don't know; I don't know; and I don't know.")

Dr. Ray: Alas, most kids do know how to take tests, so their answer is typically "D"—none of the above.

Dad: Are you afraid of what I'm going to do if you tell me why you did this? Is that it?

Dr. Ray: Dad is getting closer. In the face of *why?* kids cling to ignorance. Why?

They truly don't know. Self-insight is a quality that takes effort, willingness, and maturity—years' worth.

They do know—sort of—but they anticipate that the wrong answer could only inflame the situation. If Chip were to say, "Because I really liked Holly for about three weeks there, more than I liked our house," how likely would Dad be satisfied and declare, "Oh, all right then, that does explain it. Now go watch some TV while I scrub this off"?

A lot of what kids do is spur-of-the-moment. Meaning there's not much thinking attached to it.

Throughout this whole interchange, Dad is smacking his head against a wall, so to speak. Let's rewrite the early dialogue, or should I say, "monologue."

Dad (pointing to the carving): What is this?

Chip: I didn't think it would stay like that. I thought it would wash away.

Dr. Ray: A *what* question usually evokes more response than a *why* question. The *what* is staring both parent and child in the face. Any *why* could be hidden somewhere in the fuzzy depths of a youngster's psyche.

Dad: I'd like some explanation for this. If you give me one, it could help you out. If not, I'll just have to make my own guess about what this means.

Chip: I guess I wasn't thinking too good. Holly came by on her bike, and we were talking, and I guess I was trying to show off.

Dr. Ray: Seems pretty honest. Dad makes it clear that he isn't about to haul out the bright lights and grill for an answer. He sets up a one-question condition: Please help me understand, and it may lessen your discipline. If you can't or won't, I'll have to act "in ignorance," and that may not be in your self-interest.

Dad: OK, now, what should we do about this?

Chip (Back to silence, as if to say, "What do you mean 'we'? You're not going to scrub the siding. You're not going to have to do extra work around here.")

Dad: All right, Chip, if you don't have any ideas, I'm going to think about this awhile, and then I'll let you know what I'm going to do.

Dr. Ray: Dad doesn't struggle for a why. He asks once, then moves ahead. He uses two *what* questions: "What's this?" and "What should we do about it?" He, not Chip, controls the exchange.

He doesn't dispute Chip's *why*. He accepts it, though he might think it's incomplete or consider it a feeble attempt to maneuver around oncoming discipline. More complete *why*s sometimes emerge later, away from the pressure of the moment.

Chip (walking toward the house, looking over his shoulder): Can I just scrub off Holly's name and leave mine up there for the next girl?

Dr. Ray: OK, Chip didn't say that. I did. I thought it might be floating around somewhere inside his head.

EPILOGUE

"You're a psychologist; you should know why he did that."

Years of shrinking have humbled me. I've learned again and again that I can't always fathom every reason underlying someone's conduct, be she young or old. I may not be able to completely ferret out why a husband gambles inveterately, why a wife spends indiscriminately, or why a child overreacts emotionally, but my foremost goal is action. It is to help someone decrease the bad behavior and increase the good.

Put another way, much of child-rearing—and life—is managing behavior for the better even when one doesn't fully understand its cause.

Why is this so? I don't know. Ask Chip.

CHAPTER 19

Just Give Me One Reason

Actors: Mom; thirteen-year-old Forest; Mrs. Campio
Scene: Kitchen; family room; bathroom; car
Time: Two days prior to a possible backyard campout

PROLOGUE

When parents nag kids, we get ignored. When they nag us, we keep answering. Just who is smarter?

Forest: Hey, Mom, Mrs. Campio asked me if I wanted to camp out with Hunter in their backyard on Friday. Can I? I'll do all my school stuff today and clean up my room too, OK?

Mom: Mrs. Campio asked you? Is she going to camp out too?

Dr. Ray: Forest may be just a budding woodsman, but he's a fully grown negotiator. His gambit is to present his request as coming from a grown-up, giving it an air of added credibility and hence making it harder to refuse.

Note Forest's bonus bargaining chip: schoolwork and chores completed willingly. Since those likely are his core responsibilities, camping or no, he is really saying: I'll fulfill my duties without your having to nag me. Isn't that good of me?

Mom: Did Mrs. Campio ask you, or did Hunter?

Dr. Ray: Uh-oh. Mom isn't completely taken in by the "Mrs. Campio wants me to" maneuver, so Forest is forced to backtrack. But not all the way.

Forest: Well, I think maybe she might have told Hunter to ask me. But he said it was OK with his mom.

Mom: Did you remember you have a game on Saturday morning, and your coach wants you there by 8:30? That's trying to cram too much into one night and morning. I don't think it's a good idea this weekend. Besides, we're leaving at noon on Saturday to visit your grandparents, and it's a two-hour drive.

Forest: Mom, I'll get up. That's not hard for me. And Hunter already invited two of his other friends, maybe three. Come on, please.

Dr. Ray: The masterful "You'll be hurting other people if you refuse me." Or to say it another way, "The more others are counting on me, the more you'll be the parental killjoy if you don't cooperate."

Mom: Look, Forest, I said I don't think this weekend will work. There's too much going on. Maybe some other time.

Forest: But, Mom, it's supposed to be perfect campout weather on Friday. That's what Mrs. Campio said.

Dr. Ray: And just exactly what constitutes "perfect campout weather"? What's more, Forest may be pushing the "Mrs. Campio wants me to" a little too far.

Mom (moving into the family room with Forest tracking two steps behind her): I'm going to see if all this is Mrs. Campio's idea. Hi, Fern. Forest's mom. Forest says you were planning a campout for the boys this Friday...

Uh-huh, I see...

OK, well, we've got a lot going on this weekend, so I think we'll have to pass, but thank you for thinking of Forest. Bye.

(To Forest): She said this was Hunter's idea, and that she didn't know a whole lot about it. She said he went ahead and arranged it without checking with her, but that she didn't see a big problem with it.

Dr. Ray: Both boys seem to be claiming, "The grown-up wants this; we're just being accommodating." The phone call should close the matter, or so Mom thinks.

Forest: See? She doesn't care if we camp out. She's a really nice lady, and they always check on us before they go to bed. And Hunter's older brother might camp out with us too.

Dr. Ray: Forest is talking as if nothing is settled yet, and for good measure he cites how agreeable and responsible that other parent is.

Mom: You are just not letting this go, are you? I said, not this weekend. It's too full.

Forest: But, Mom, I have games almost every Saturday. It'll just be the same every time I want to camp out.

Mom (heading into the bathroom, seeking sanctuary): Forest, you're not going to get anywhere by hounding me. You can nag all you want; my answer will still be the same.

Forest (from the other side of the bathroom door): I just don't understand why I can't go. There's no good reason. It's just one night, and I'll come home in the morning, ready to go to the game. Mrs. Campio will bring me back.

Dr. Ray: When a kid claims, "I just don't understand," it's a pretty good indication he perfectly well understands. He just doesn't agree or like his parent's reasoning. Nonetheless, many parents feel compelled to explain until a child does understand. Soon they will experience the law of diminishing returns: Over-reasoning leads to more arguing and more agitation—in short, less "understanding."

Forest: Aren't you going to answer me? Why can't I go this one time if I promise to come back early on Saturday? I even play ball better when I'm a little tired. I'm not as nervous.

Mom: Oh, come on. Why don't you just fall asleep during the game? Then you'll be really relaxed and can play your best. I told you, Forest, drop it. All your arguing is not going to work.

Forest: I'm not arguing. I'm just trying to talk to you about this. Why won't you listen to what I'm saying?

Dr. Ray: "Why won't you listen?" is a variant of "I don't understand." Mom has been listening, one could argue, for too long. "Why won't you listen?" often means "Why aren't you seeing this my way?" Forest isn't ready to pack it in until Mom hits her emotional limit.

Mom (heading out the door to the car, to run errands and to seek the peace that dwells in the distance): Forest, that's enough. All your nagging is only making me mad. If you want to ever have a chance to camp out, you'd better let this go. Now, get away from the car. I have to go. And do *not* call me after I leave.

Forest (stepping back): Great. Not only can't I be with my friends on Friday, but now you're telling me I can never be with them. I don't even care if I play baseball. It wrecks everything.

Dr. Ray: Forest's *camp de graux*—a last-ditch delivery of guilt and apathy wrapped in accusation. One hopes Mom has the window rolled up, with the radio tuned to a rock station on full volume, singing along with gusto.

EPILOGUE

Two streams of futility emerge in this scenario. The first is Mom's explaining herself long after it becomes obvious that Forest isn't about to be persuaded. Every answer she offers only meets more counter-answers from Forest, mostly unreasonable ones, the most creative being the psychologically tinged, "I play less nervous when I'm tired."

Much earlier in the exchange, Mom could reasonably have said something like, "Forest, I gave you my reasons. You didn't like any of them. Now, please, another argument, and you're in your room."

or,

"One more word, and the next time you want to camp out, the answer will be an automatic no."

or,

"Forest, you nag me again, and you'll write a three-hundred-word essay on why my reasons are good ones."

Would this be an autocratic stifling of open parent-child "dialogue"? Not at all. One, it is not much of a dialogue; it is an argument, stoked by Forest. Clearly he has no intention of forging a mutual meeting of the minds.

Two, when an open dialogue turns disagreeable, it's time to close it—fast. Or else it almost always deteriorates. Witness Mom's departure in frustration and Forest's farewell nastiness.

The second stream of futility involves Mom's determination not to be nagged into submission. She feels she can resist all of Forest's best efforts ("You can say all you want; my answer will still be the same"), but the campout is still two days away. That's thirty-plus hours of potential hounding, not counting sleep time, though I wouldn't put it past Forest to figure out how to subliminally harass Mom while she's unconscious.

Mom may be able to endure Forest's badgering, but why should she have to? At the least it's aggravating. At the most it's challenging her authority, as Forest is refusing to accept her decision. Parents will assert, "I stand my ground and don't yield to all the nagging." Perhaps, but they still are submitting themselves to it, lots of it.

A simple rule: Once your decision is made, permit no more nagging. It only agitates all parties and results in more discord per nag.

My wife has a pet phrase: Are you nagging? Meaning: Cease now, or there will be consequences. And more often than I can count, I respond, "OK, but just let me say one more thing...."

CHAPTER 20

Let's Not Quibble About This

Actors: Dad; Mom; fourteen-year-old Perry; twelve-year-old Mason

Scene: Kitchen; stairwell; upstairs hallway; bedroom

Time: 7:22 PM and later

PROLOGUE

Adolescents are notorious for not talking much to parents. But when they're facing discipline, the words pour out. The goal is to bury parents in irrelevancies.

Perry (entering the house with his brother, Mason, at exactly 7:22 PM): Hey, Mom, we're home. Thanks for letting us go to the pool today. It was a really great time.

Mason: Yeah, thanks. It was so cool. Probably the best fun we had there this summer.

Dr. Ray: Were the boys coming home from a typical afternoon at the pool, one might be impressed with their cheery greetings. Such manners, coupled with gratitude—a winning entrance aimed at setting a positive tone. It happens, though, that the boys are moseying in nearly one and a half hours past the 6:00 PM "be home" time. And Grandma's birthday party started at 7:00 PM at her house.

Dad (sipping coffee at the kitchen table, noticeably irritated): What time were you boys told to be home?

Perry: I think maybe you said somewhere around six or so. Mason heard you too.

Mason: Yeah, you didn't give an exact time. You kind of said, "Just don't be late." And we're not really that late.

Dr. Ray: When staring trouble in the face, get fuzzy. String together as many qualifiers as can be packed into a few sentences: I think... maybe...somewhere around...or so...kind of. If possible, cite an "ear witness"—"Mason heard you too"—along with the silent plea, "Mason, help me out here."

Mom: Yes, we did give you an exact time. We told you to be home no later than six. You need time to shower and get ready.

Mason: We don't need that much time. We're not girls. I can clean up in a few minutes. So can Perry.

Dr. Ray: The first quibble misstep. Stick to fudging the facts; don't insert potentially ruffling social commentary, especially to Mom, who is a girl. Mason, being twelve, is less smooth than Perry. Typically, the older the child, the more sophisticated the quibbling. A benefit of experience. Perry quickly tries to regain footing.

Perry: We'd have been here sooner, but Webb's mom got there late to pick us up.

Mason: That's right. We didn't know if she'd come on time 'cause she does come late sometimes.

Dr. Ray: Perry's reasoning is a staple of teenagers. When arriving an hour or more late, cite something that delayed you six minutes, using it to account for most of your tardiness.

Mason is in the role of echo quibbler. In case Perry's clouding of events isn't cloudy enough, he'll reiterate, along with releasing a few clouds of his own: "...'cause she does come late sometimes."

Dad: We called Webb's house at 6:15, and his dad told us Mrs.

Webb left to get you a few minutes after six. It's no more than a ten-minute drive.

Perry: Not all the time. That's only if there's no traffic. But like you always say, the roads get full around this time, especially on Friday. Besides, the pool was so crowded, Mrs. Webb had to park at the back of the lot, and we had to walk to her car. She didn't pick us up at the gate like she mostly does.

Mom: The parking lot isn't that big. You can walk the whole thing in a couple of minutes.

Mason: Sometimes you can. But today there were a lot of people swimming.

Dad: What does that have to do with anything?

Perry: Well, if you have people in front of you moving slow, with little kids, it's hard to go around them when you're in a hurry, like we were.

Dr. Ray: Perry jumps in quickly to rescue Mason, as he hears him drifting. But his answer is shallow too, so Mason swims in a different direction.

Mason: I don't think Mrs. Webb got there by 6:15. I looked at the pool clock, and it said 6:20, and she wasn't there yet.

Mom: That concession stand clock is set ten minutes fast, and you know it. They want to close the pool every night a few minutes early. Besides, we saw Mrs. Webb pull into her driveway at 6:20. That was over an hour ago. Where were you all this time?

Dr. Ray: The boys are exchanging looks. The last thing they need at this point is to present conflicting accounts. An axiom of quibbling: Stay vague, but stay consistently vague.

Mom and Dad sound determined to get to the bottom of all this. The problem is, the boys are just as determined to offer no bottom. Dad, out of frustration or exhaustion, abandons pursuit—and abandons Mom—heading up the stairs. Bounding three steps behind, seeing his out, is Mason.

Mason: I can get ready real fast, Dad. I'm pretty much the fastest shower-taker I know. (Dr. Ray translation: See, Dad, you don't have to think anymore about punishing me because I'm about to make it all right.)

Perry (answering Mom's "Where were you all this time?"): Well, when we finally got back, Mrs. Webb asked us to help her carry the swimming stuff into her house, and then when we came out, Mr. Goodman saw us—you know, their neighbor, that really nice guy you said you liked, and he likes you too. He asked us to come over and see his new Jet Ski. We didn't want to be rude, so we went over for a few minutes.

Dr. Ray: A master in action. Wherever able, add sidebars that appeal to a parent. I mean, who can argue with being polite and neighborly to a "really nice guy," one who likes you, no less?

Mom: And just what do you call a few minutes? That was still an hour ago. How long does it take to look at a Jet Ski?

Perry: Well, Mr. Goodman was excited to show it to us, and he asked all three of us to sit on it. And he said he'd take us out sometime on it. He likes to talk a lot.

Dr. Ray: Perry is desperately trying to account for the last minutes but is running out of time. Time to throw little brother under the bus or, if you will, into the pool.

Perry: I was ready to come home, but Mason went back in the house with Webb. I don't know what they were doing in there. I waited a long time before he came back out.

Mom: You could have just gone in and gotten him. You didn't have to just sit there and wait. You knew you were already late.

Perry: I know, but I didn't know we were that late. There's no clock in Mr. Goodman's garage.

Dr. Ray: The only thing more exasperating than listening to this kind of quibble bout is being a partner to it. Perry will go on until Grandma's next birthday party if he has to. He has everything to gain and little to lose. However he can, he must muddy the waters sufficiently to cause Mom self-doubt about any discipline. Or should he be disciplined, at the least he can salvage an "unjustly accused" status.

Dad (from upstairs bedroom): Perry, are you going to get up here and clean up? The shower is open. Let's go!

Perry: OK, Dad. I'm coming up right now. I won't take long at all to get ready. Thanks, Mom. I'll be down in a few minutes.

Dr. Ray: Unwittingly, Dad gave Perry the escape he was angling for. Leaving Mom standing wordless, he shoots up the stairs in full cooperation mode. "Thanks, Mom." What does that mean? Perhaps, "For understanding." Or, "For hearing me out…and out…and out." Most likely it means, "For not doing anything about this."

Mom (to a rapidly retreating Perry): Hurry up. Aunt Patience called right at seven to ask where we were.

Dr. Ray: Johnny Carson is said to have advised: Don't share the spotlight with kids or animals. They'll upstage you every time. That's sound advice for parents: Don't try to out-quibble a quibbler. He will bury you in his words and tangle you in his logic.

EPILOGUE

When discipline looms, kids gravitate toward one of two poles. One, shut up and stare. Say not a word, nothing to self-incriminate.

Two, start talking, and fast. Debate any and every particular that comes to mind. And use a parent's points as fodder for more counterpoints.

A veteran quibbler also knows to sprinkle his defense with evidence of social positives, such as good manners and eagerness to cooperate. This breaks up an otherwise continuous string of objections that might quickly irritate the parent.

Defense attorneys aim to foster as much doubt about a case as the judge allows. Kids could teach Perry Mason a thing or two. The goal of an elite quibbler is to create (a) uncertainty, (b) confusion, (c) fatigue, (d) a pardon from discipline, or (e) all of the above.

So how can a parent shut down quibbling? The solution is straightforward: Identify the process early, and then pull its plug. Let's return to Perry's first couple of quibbles.

Perry: We'd have been here sooner, but Webb's mom got there late to pick us up.

Dad: Perry, we know what time Webb's mom got there. We called Mrs. Webb. So let's not start arguing picky details. That'll just tempt you to dig yourself a deeper hole.

Mom: We're not going to quibble about this any further. We still have to decide what to do about it, but for now, go upstairs and clean up. You've got ten minutes.

Dr. Ray: Is this squashing a child's right to "be heard"? Not at all. First, he can make his case later if he wishes, post-discipline. Not too many do—which tells us something about motives.

Second, if a youngster does have a legitimate point, such as, "Mrs. Webb made us wash and wax her car before she'd bring us home," it can be considered. Most parents can discriminate between the verbal wheat and verbal chaff.

Last, and most often, a youngster's primary intent is not to be heard. It is to state, restate, and then state again his position. Or to state it differently, quibbling doesn't open up communication; it closes it.

For the sake of all involved, a wise parent stifles quibbling fast. Once quibble number 2 has been reached, quibbles 3 through infinity almost always follow.

Of politics it's been said, if you can't win them over with facts, baffle them with baloney. I wonder, How old was the child who first advised that?

CHAPTER 21

A Rolling Rebuttal

Actors: Mom; Dad; fourteen-year-old Felicity
Scene: Kitchen; stairs; hallway; bedroom
Time: Late Saturday morning

PROLOGUE
Disrespect comes with many faces. Sometimes what's unspoken speaks louder than any words.

Mom: Felicity, would you come up here, please?
Felicity: Why? What do you need me for?
Mom: Just come up here, please.
Dr. Ray: When a youngster answers a parent with a "Why?" or a "What?" that usually signals she doesn't think she needs to cooperate just yet. Rather, she thinks she deserves a more acceptable explanation. A "Why?" is seldom a true request for a *why*. It is an opening to dispute the reasonableness of the parent's request or command.

Felicity's mother doesn't explain any further; she's likely learned that confronting Felicity face-to-face in her bedroom is better than arguing with her from one floor up.

Suppose Felicity's mom were to offer, "Why? Because your room is a mess, and you need to clean it before you do anything else today." Would she hear Felicity bounding up the stairs two at a time, declaring breathlessly at the top, "Gee, Mother, why didn't you just say that's why you wanted me up here so quickly?" Let's conduct a test to find out.

Mom: Why? Because your room is a mess, and you need to clean it before you do anything else.

Felicity (stomping up the stairs one at a time, to maximize her footstep commentary): I cleaned it right after I got up. It's not that bad. Just a couple pairs of jeans on the bed. It's my room; why can't I keep it the way I want?

Mom: Whose room are you looking at? There are three pairs of jeans under the bed alone.

Dr. Ray: In eyeballing the condition of a teen's bedroom, many parents wonder not what room their teen inhabits but what planet. How is it that she can gaze straight at the disarray and rotting debris and deny reality? What's more, didn't she confront all this when she scrounged for some clothes to wear today? Does she really not observe what we observe, or is she pleading some sort of Fifth Amendment defense: "I'm sorry. I don't recall seeing what you're saying."

"It's my room" is true in a limited sense. The teen does occupy it, usually for several years, and maybe later in young adulthood if he moves back home. But that room resides within a parent's house, and as landlord, the parent has every right to determine reasonable terms of occupancy, if nothing else but to minimize the depreciation in value to the whole house.

As Mom continues to assert her wishes, the interchange goes much more sour.

Mom: Well, whatever you think, I think it needs to be picked up. So you might as well stay in here until it looks right.

Felicity (with an emphatic rolling of the eyes): Whatever.

Mom: Get started. I told you, you are not doing anything else until this room is clean.

Felicity (More eye rolls, some sighs, with a half-smirk, as if to say, "Keep talking, Stress Mom.")

Mom: And I don't need to see any of your nasty looks either, young lady. I won't tolerate them.

Dr. Ray: Whatever Mom is meaning to say with "I won't tolerate them," she is in fact tolerating them, as she has yet to do anything about them except say she won't tolerate them.

As commonly happens, the initial discipline subject—here, a disordered room—is being superseded by a more serious piece of misconduct—disrespect, however wordless.

Felicity (While throwing clothes in a pile on the bed, throws Mom one more over-the-shoulder scowl that nonverbally communicates, in essence, "I can't believe you.")

Mom: You know, Felicity, you have a real attitude problem anytime I ask you to do something you don't like. You'd better get yourself under control.

Felicity (One final shaking of the head, as if to say, "What's your problem?")

Mom (stomping out of the room and down the stairs, doing her own footstep commentary): There are going to be some changes around here. I have had my fill of her attitude. I have let it go on way too long, and it's going to stop. She'll find that out.

Dr. Ray: Call what Mom is doing "self" discipline. It's a lecture to herself and the nearby air, hoping that some bit of it will register in a child's ears. In its effects it is similar to talking to a nearby wall.

Despite Felicity's eight or nine—depending on how they are tallied—disdainful and disgusted back looks, Mom, while noticeably upset, takes no action. True, she does reiterate her unwillingness to allow disrespect even as she allows it, but no actual discipline occurs.

Dad (arriving home from running an errand): Hi, Honey. How is your morning going? Looks like you didn't get a chance to pick up the house yet, huh?

Dr. Ray: We'd better yell "Cut" here. Something tells me what's coming may need some heavy editing.

EPILOGUE

Two subplots are intertwined in this episode—a dirty room and dirty looks. As with many discipline scenarios, where the trouble began isn't where it ended. Things started out benign enough: Please clean your room. Felicity escalated the interchange to a level more serious: disrespect.

Let's tidy up the room first. Mom's initial idea was elegantly simple: The room must be picked up before any privileges begin. This is a basic operating rule for keeping a teen's turf under ten violations of the city's health code. Upon picking up the first back look, Mom could have added a condition.

Mom: Felicity, if you're that unhappy about cleaning your room, you don't have to. I can do it for you. I'll need to get a big trash bag. I don't really know what to throw out and what to keep, but if stuff is on the floor, I may just assume you don't care about it.

Dr. Ray: No sarcasm, no threat, just a quiet, resolute statement of intent.

But don't some experts assert: A child has the right to keep "her room" as she wishes? This expert agrees, if the parent agrees. If not, the parent's wishes—not to mention her duty to teach responsibility—would seem to supersede any expert-afforded "right" to a ruined room.

Now, on to the weightier matter: Felicity's facial commentary. Why would Mom essentially overlook such mistreatment? A couple of possibilities.

One, in the words of a song, "I've grown accustomed to her face. It almost makes the day begin." Because Felicity so regularly puts her worst face forward, Mom has been desensitized. She now needs several rapid-fire images in a row to become aware of what's being directed her way.

Two, Mom has resigned herself to another notion fostered by experts: Back looks are just teens being teens. They are a natural part of the adolescent persona and as such should be endured until the face grows up. After all, there is no verbal ugliness, screaming, or throwing of bricks. Pick your battles.

Let's do another test. Choose a close someone—best friend, employer, pastor, judge—and for the next month or so, make sure you show that person visually whenever you disagree with him or her. At month's end ask, "Do you still like me?" See if the person affirms you with, "Well, I have noticed you've been more open with your authentic self, and I am learning to appreciate it." Or will you need to find a new friend, new church, new job, or new lawyer?

Back looks are disrespect. They convey, "That is ridiculous." Or worse, "You are ridiculous." Therefore, Mom would do well to face them down firmly at first sight.

Mom: Felicity, all I did was ask you nicely to pick up your room, and you got rude. So now your room will be cleaned by you—or by me and my bag—and even after it's done, you will go nowhere today.

Dr. Ray: Is all this because one rolling of the eyes is so bad? Not necessarily. It is because a good mom—or dad—is so valuable.

CHAPTER 22

Battered Parent Syndrome

Actors: Mom; fourteen-year-old Joy; Mom's friend Patsy
Scene: School cafeteria
Time: Wednesday at 7:45 PM

PROLOGUE

A teen can so routinely mistreat a parent that the parent no longer notices. That's not good for the parent or the teen.

Joy: Mom, are you about ready to go yet? How long is this going to take? We've already been here a half an hour more than you said.

Mom: I know, Honey. This is taking a little longer than I thought it would. Patsy and I just have a few more details to add to the flyer, and then we're done. It should only be about fifteen more minutes.

Joy: Fifteen more minutes!? You said that a half hour ago! I never would have come if it was going to take this long. Bliss and her mom left a long time ago. We're the only ones left.

Mom: They did?

Joy: Yes, they did!

Mom: Well, I guess their part of the program was done. Be patient. We won't be too much longer. Why don't you stack up some of the extra flyers from last year?

Joy: Bliss and I already did that. Now I'm stuck here with nothing to do. I could have stayed home. At least I could have done my hair and not had to sit here all night.

WINNING THE DISCIPLINE DEBATES

Mom: Please, Joy. I'm trying to hurry.

Joy: Give me the keys. Just give me the keys. I'll be in the car, and then you can take all the time you want.

Mom: They're in my purse.

Dr. Ray: About the only thing nastier than Joy's words is her demeanor. She's telling Mom in no uncertain tone that she is being quite inconvenienced. Mom, however, sounds blissfully unaware of how she's being treated. Joy is barking at Mom, and Mom is singing "Kumbaya."

Mom (to Patsy): Sorry about all that. She was starting to get disrespectful, so I'm glad she's heading for the car.

Patsy: That's all right. That's pretty normal for kids her age. You should hear my daughter when she's on a roll. Yours was pretty mild.

Dr. Ray: Starting to get disrespectful? Joy started right out disrespectful. In fact, she started out near full throttle. Mom's friend is trying to be a friend, but she speaks through some common misconceptions.

It may be typical ("normal") for adolescents to get surly (it becomes much more normal if allowed); it isn't good. Mouthiness may peak in the teen years, but it best not be endured because it "happens at that age." Two-year-olds throw volcanic meltdowns. Should a parent chalk it up to the "terrible twos" and cover her head until it passes? That's a lot of ash falling on everyone.

Because Joy isn't as rude as Patsy's daughter is no consolation to Mom. It's not hard to find kids more trouble than one's own. Mom's sole concern is that *her* daughter is rude. Because Patsy's daughter is so inclined does nothing to lessen Joy's ill conduct.

Mom: She's so much quicker to get upset with me than she used to be. I'll admit, I let a lot if it pass because there's so much of it. Joy doesn't do this at school or with any of her friends or her father. It's only me. I think we're too much alike.

Patsy: Angel and I get into it a lot too. My husband says the same thing: Our personalities are too much alike. We butt heads.

Dr. Ray: Whether or not either mom realizes it, they've just insulted themselves. What exactly is a parent saying by saying that she doesn't get along with a child because she's too much like that child? That child is difficult, and so am I? In short, to assert that one is too much like a child might be implying one is childish.

A strong parent doesn't battle a youngster at her level—word for word, tone for tone, argument for argument. Mom needs to reassess and reestablish her authority.

Mom: My mother has asked me a bunch of times, "Do you hear how she is talking to you?" Maybe I've gotten so used to it that it doesn't even register anymore. It does seem to take more and more to make me wake up to it.

Patsy: That's easy to let happen. My older son really had a bad attitude, and I remember so many times thinking later, "Why did I let him get away with talking like that?" But usually that was after the fight passed, and I just wanted peace.

Dr. Ray: I label this dynamic the "Battered Parent Syndrome." Mom and/or Dad have allowed themselves to be so regularly mistreated that, as with a bad drug, they've developed tolerance for the mistreatment. The child has to nearly curse or throw chairs before the parent hears it, and by then both are so incensed that any discipline is flung angrily and received even more angrily.

Patsy: What do you think you'll run into when you get out to the car? Do you think she'll still be mad?

Mom: Probably. But at least if it's a cold mad, I'll have some quiet. I'm just hoping she doesn't start up again. I'm getting tired of those kinds of car rides.

Dr. Ray: Mom doesn't need to live dreading Joy's moods or the car rides. She is the parent. She is the one to set, or to settle, the tone of an exchange. If Joy accelerates her grumpiness the instant Mom puts the vehicle in drive, Mom can immediately put on the brakes, figuratively or literally. She can tell Joy exactly what discipline awaits her, not only for starting up again but because of her scene thirty-four minutes before.

EPILOGUE

Being a long-time clinician has given me a long time to ponder many questions. One is: Why are so many kids so free to talk so disrespectfully to parents, and why are parents so free to accept it? One answer: A bevy of child-rearing "experts" (I use that word carefully) insist that children should be allowed to "express" themselves. The psychologically unenlightened parent risks raising a youngster who becomes an automaton Stepford child, thinking, "Yes, Mother (Father), on the outside I will respect you, but on the inside I can't stomach you."

Children do have definite opinions about our parenting—after all, it's what affects their lives most definitely. Giving and receiving those opinions make for a healthy, two-way relationship. Healthy, that is, as long as the opinions are presented respectfully. License to express does not mean license to mistreat. Sharing sentiments and showing disrespect are mutually exclusive. One is open communication with parents; the other is open season on parents.

How then does a parent sensitize himself to something he has been insensitive to, perhaps for quite a while? There is a simple test. Ask yourself: If these words, tones, or looks came from another adult, how would I react? Bad expressions are expressions that damage relationships, kid to grown-up, grown-up to kid, or grown-up to grown-up.

An invaluable gift of parenting: We can always reassess our ways, and we can correct what we find needs correction. If you have allowed too much "open communication," you can always communicate what the new, more aware you is about.

Let's give Mom a more pleasant last half hour at her meeting:

Joy: Mom, are you about ready to go yet? How long is this going to take? We've already been here a half an hour more than you said.

Mom: Yes, we have, and, Joy, you need to settle down. If you can't, you will wait in the car, without the keys [that is, no radio]. Any more of that tone, and I will do something about it when we get home. Now, please apologize to Mrs. Flowers.

Dr. Ray: Embarrassing for Joy? Probably. It would be even more embarrassing for Mom and Mrs. Flowers (Patsy) to allow Joy to keep talking.

Will Joy regroup simply because Mom warned her to? Probably not. But Mom has voiced a precedent. Disrespect is disrespect, whenever and wherever it begins.

CHAPTER 23

A Brave New World

Actors: Mom; Dad; fourteen-year-old Cellina
Scene: Mom and Dad's bedroom
Time: Parents' bedtime

PROLOGUE

Cell phones have altered—for better or for worse—the way everyone, adult or child, lives. On balance, they are not a friend to parents, or to kids for that matter. As for giving a cell phone to one's offspring, the later the better.

Cellina (entering parents' bedroom, where parents are in bed but awake): Do either of you know where my cell phone is? Tomorrow's the day you said I'd get it back, and I want to have it tonight so I don't have to ask for it in the morning.

Dad: Yes, we know where it is. We were going to talk to you about that tomorrow. Mom and I have made a decision about your cell phone.

Cellina: What do you mean? You said I'd only lose it for a week. I'm not going to use it tonight. I won't even turn it on, but I do have to have it early tomorrow.

Mom: That's just the point. Why do you have to have it first thing in the morning? We've been thinking a lot more about this whole cell phone thing, and we're thinking it was a bad idea.

Cellina (moving closer to the bed): What!? I do one thing wrong, and I lose my cell for good? You said you were only going to take it for one week.

Dr. Ray: To use terms of communication theory, Cellina is in a "one up" position. Mom and Dad are lying prone in bed; Cellina is standing—one might say towering—over them. She may lack domestic authority, but unconsciously she's asserting postural authority. The folks may just be too tired to pursue equal footing.

Mom: Cellina, this isn't the best time to talk about this. It's getting late. We can go over all our reasons tomorrow.

Cellina (more agitated): Go over all your reasons tomorrow?! I said "I'm sorry" for texting in bed, and I accepted my punishment. What else do I have to do to get my phone back?

Dr. Ray: Want to gauge how linked to a cell phone a youngster is? Want to measure how indispensable she considers it to her social well-being? Listen to her desperation at the mere thought of its absence, not just temporarily but indefinitely. Cellina's poor reception of her parents' message is compelling her to keep this interchange going, as she can't possibly sleep with this horrid possibility still lingering.

Dad: It's not a question of when you can have your phone back. It's more than that. Mom and I agree on this. That thing has become way too important to you. We think we let you have one too soon.

Cellina: Too soon! Too soon? I got mine way later than my friends did. They all had theirs two or three years before me. And they do all kinds of wrong stuff with theirs. I don't.

Dr. Ray: Careful, Cellina. Whether you realize it or not, you're making the case that cell phones are major temptations to social misconduct for many kids.

Despite wanting to delay until tomorrow the gory details of their decision, Mom and Dad are getting pulled in tonight. It's highly unlikely tomorrow will dawn with a mutual meeting of the minds; such a meeting is nearly impossible tonight. Yet unless they order Cellina to bed, she's not about to hang this up. Her parents' unexpected call is way too critical for her to go quietly into that good night.

Cellina: OK, I won't be on my phone as much, and I'll slow my texting down. Come on, please. That's how all my friends get hold of me. That's how we all talk now.

Dr. Ray: Yeah, you pre-Bell relics. How do you expect kids to have any kind of friendships without a cell phone?

Dad: Yes, Cellina, that *is* how you and your friends connect now. And that's the problem. You may talk to your friends on the phone more, but you talk to people around you less. And heaven forbid if someone texts you in the middle of anything else you're doing. You feel as if you have to drop what you're doing and answer the person. At Grandma's birthday party last week, you barely talked to anyone there, because every two minutes somebody made your phone buzz.

Dr. Ray: One survey found that the typical adolescent sends and receives up to three thousand texts per month. That's a hundred per day, more in February! Personally, I'm aware of kids whose total dwarfs that.

Is texting in and of itself such a social ill? Not necessarily. Being ever on call to the techno-world is. Teens are social creatures, and the reachability offered by a constant phone companion provides a minute-by-minute temptation toward excess, an excess that can crowd out other communication—like, U know, talking to people personally and stuff. LOL.

Cellina: Dad, the reason I was on my phone at Grandma's was because I had to know what the science assignment was. I had a project due that week, and Newton was helping me with it. I got a B+ because I knew what Mr. Cosmos wanted.

Dr. Ray: The logic is unassailable: cell phone=better grade. Hear, too, how Cellina refers to it as "my phone." When I was a kid, back in the Cenozoic era, we called our landline "the phone," as in, "I'm on the phone." It was an impersonal device. Not so anymore.

Cellina: Besides, how can you know when to pick me up after soccer practice? It doesn't always end at the same time. And you always say you feel better when I have my phone with me, in case of an emergency or something.

Mom: You're right. And we've thought about that. Either you can take one of our phones if you need to, or we'll get you one with limited minutes and no texting.

Dad: If, as you say, all of your friends have cell phones, you can just use one of theirs.

Cellina: Oh, great. Now I'll be known as the mooch who has to borrow everybody else's things. I just don't get this. I haven't done anything all that wrong, and I'm still being really punished. This is totally unfair.

Mom: Now, you know as well as we do, Cellina, that you have misused that cell phone. Some texts you've gotten were pretty crude. And you returned a few the same way. You've been caught more than once on that phone after hours, and we really have no idea who you talk to. All this has convinced Dad and me that it was not a good idea to let you have a cell phone yet. I'll admit, we gave in to the pressure, from you and everybody else. But we've changed our minds. We're allowed to do that.

Dr. Ray: Yes, you are. Parents make all kinds of judgments that later need to be adjusted, even reversed. When a parent realizes that she has allowed too much freedom too early, in any area—computer, peers, media, dating, driving—she has the right, indeed the duty, to change course. Sometimes this involves not just temporarily removing a privilege; it involves deciding that the privilege shouldn't have been granted in the first place.

Cellina: The only reason you know about those texts is that you went into my phone looking for something bad. I can't believe you'd go into my private texts.

Dad: Well, believe it. Where your safety and morals are concerned, we will always check up on you. And don't try to make us feel guilty. We're glad we checked.

Dr. Ray: The right to privacy is a guiding principle in law. It's a misguiding principle in parenting. A parent's primary responsibility is to protect a child, from herself if need be. According to Cellina, the texts weren't as wrong as was her parents' looking for them. Mom and Dad are wise to resist such sophistry. The "right" to privacy is trumped by a more basic right—the right of a parent to know what is going on in a child's life.

Cellina: How long will it be before I get my phone back? I might as well just forget about having friends.

Mom: Come on, Cellina, we're not getting anywhere. We'll talk more about this tomorrow. Now, good night. We love you.

Cellina (No "good night," no kiss; a silent turn and exit).

Dad (to Mom): I knew that phone was attached to her ear, but I never realized how much. I think it's going to be cool around here for a while.

Mom: Even if it is, we've got to hold our ground. We saw what happened. It was too much of an intrusion into our family. It was her priority, and it pushed other people, like us and her brother, into the background. No, we did the right thing.

Dad: I know, but we'd better brace ourselves for this topic to come up again and again. For how long, who knows?

Mom: No. We can tell her tomorrow that if she doesn't let this go, it will only push back the age she finally does get one. And she'll lose other freedoms as well. She is going to have to live with this.

Dr. Ray: If Cellina thought her parents were two generations out of touch before this ruling, she'll think they're Neanderthals now. But good parents make decisions based upon their merits, not upon what a child thinks of them. What's more, as Mom and Dad bring more balance into their daughter's life, they will be ever more convinced they made the right call. And Cellina will probably still have friends. Almost all teens have had friends, even prior to personal phones.

EPILOGUE

Thirty years as a shrink can radically shift how one thinks. And I have become ever more convinced that giving an adolescent, much less a preadolescent, unlimited cell phone access is, in the main, a major mistake. Certain risks are obvious: obscene or crude messages (sexting), forming "deep" romances over the air, cheating at school, contact with peers that parents wouldn't want within an area code of their child in person. The probability of some or all of these, given time and opportunity, is significant. And too many parents have awakened to these dangers after they've happened.

While some teens can successfully navigate these temptations, for many a subtle transformation occurs. As Cellina's parents realized, Cellina's cell world intruded relentlessly into her broader world. Conversations, activities, and social connections always faced interruption, apparently by something more "urgent." Cellina felt the need to be "in contact" anytime and anywhere with whomever. Not all kids drift to this extreme, but many do. And it often happens too gradually to be noticed early on by a parent.

Safety, supervision, contact, emergency—all are cited by both kids and grown-ups as rationales for full cell access. Kids tout these rationales because they persuade parents. Parents, alas, sometimes accept them as justifications to yield to a phone when they'd really rather not. They also don't relish an ongoing "When, then?" battle.

Cellina's parents had an answer for securing the benefits without the liabilities: Purchase a phone with limited monthly minutes and no texting (OK, maybe twenty a month). Or program a few select numbers into the phone—Mom, Dad, home, police, pizza. Or have one phone for all the kids, to be used by each as necessary. Dad's solution was classic: If everyone around you has one, you don't need one.

At what age do I think a child should be given his own phone? As with any privilege of growing up, age isn't the deciding factor; moral maturity and trustworthiness are. How about a cell phone as a wedding present? Just kidding. Sort of.

My wife and I have ten children, ages eleven to twenty-four. (For confirmation, text me at my website.) A rule that has served us well: No cell until college, or eighteen if appropriately responsible.

It's become more difficult to enforce over the years. Andrew, age twenty-four, was content to get his phone sometime in college. Elizabeth, age eleven, started asking for hers in the first grade. But it was toward the end of the year.

CHAPTER 24

No Apologies for Mercy

Actors: Mom; fifteen-year-old Mercy
Scene: Mercy's bedroom; family room
Time: 8:20 PM; three weeks later

PROLOGUE

An apology doesn't show parental weakness or inconsistency. It shows parental confidence and strength. A good apology is for disciplining badly. It is not for the discipline itself.

Mom (entering Mercy's bedroom): You've been up here awhile. Are you thinking of just going to bed?

Mercy: I don't know. Maybe.

Mom: You look as if you're still really upset.

Mercy: Wouldn't you be?

Mom: Yes, I probably would. And that's why I came up here. I wanted to tell you I'm sorry. I'm sorry that I lost my temper and said some things I didn't mean at all. My emotions got the best of me. And for sure, I shouldn't have cursed at you.

Mercy (Sitting on the edge of her bed; silently staring at the floor).

Mom: I mean it. I'm really sorry for letting myself get so carried away. I was wrong.

Mercy: Yeah, OK.

Dr. Ray: In Mercy's mind it's neither "Yeah" nor "OK." Her words are more of an unspoken "Whatever." A risk of any apology—from parent to child, spouse to spouse, anyone to anyone—is rejection. It could be heard as insincere, incomplete, manipulative, too little too late, yeah-OK-whatever.

Nonetheless, an apology for a wrong is right, no matter how it is received.

Mom: You don't sound too accepting of this.

Mercy: Well, I just lost the computer for one month because you don't like what I put on my Facebook. Does "sorry" mean I get the computer back?

Mom: No. It means I'm sorry for how I acted. I'm not sorry for the discipline. Your Facebook page is totally a privilege. It's to be used responsibly. If you misuse it, you will lose it, like any privilege. This time around it's only gone for a month. If something like this happens again, it could be gone indefinitely.

Dr. Ray: Kids want to think "I'm sorry" means (1) "for how I acted" and (2) "for my discipline." They are mistaken. An apology for harsh words and emotions is unrelated to the discipline itself. The apology is for wrong conduct. Good discipline—even when levied with an ugly style—is right conduct. It is not an apology-worthy offense.

Mercy: You're "sorry" would mean more to me if you realized that taking away my computer time makes me madder than your yelling and calling me a name. Why won't you say sorry about that?

Mom: Because I'm not sorry about taking away your computer. Good discipline is not a sin. If I get mean when I discipline, well then, I'm wrong. And that's what I'm sorry for.

Mercy (Shaking her head slowly, as if to say, "Whatever makes you happy.")

Dr. Ray: Never let a youngster's possible reaction to an apology silence the apology. It's her misunderstanding, or her rejection of the discipline, or her youth that is shaping her reaction.

Then too, some kids can't pass up the chance to dispense a little punishment of their own—a payback if you will—for what in their eyes was not only undeserved treatment but, more so, undeserved discipline.

I'm sorry for repeating myself, but an apology is good self-discipline, even when rebuffed. Even when it risks making the whole discipline episode temporarily more inflamed.

Three weeks later Mercy is alone in the family room watching television. It's hard to calculate which steals more family time—the TV or the computer.

Mom: Mercy, turn the TV off, please. I want to tell you something. (Mercy obliges.)

You have been very pleasant the last three weeks. You took your computer punishment without arguing, and overall, your attitude has been beautiful. So I talked it over with Dad, and we both decided to suspend the rest of your punishment. You can have your Facebook back, starting tomorrow, the condition being that you put nothing on there that is unacceptable. We'll be keeping a closer eye on you than before, but we think you're ready to try again.

Mercy: Is this because you still feel bad about the big fight we had, when you apologized?

Mom: That's not it at all. It's because you have been very good about all this. Not once did you have a "put-upon, victim" attitude. That made a big difference in our decision.

Mercy: Well, I still wasn't happy about it.

Mom: I didn't think you were, but you kept it to yourself, and you kept it under control.

Dr. Ray: And sometimes that's the best a parent can hope for. The first step to a changed attitude is changed conduct, even if it's forced.

EPILOGUE

A parent's apology and a child's attitude are related. An apology—even when initially falling on hardened ears—can soften a child over time and yield an eventual softening of attitude. The apology reveals that the parent is not an autocrat—"My way or the highway, kid"—but one who is willing to separate parental misconduct from parental discipline. It emphasizes that discipline is meant to teach morals and character. It is not motivated by anger, nor is it a justification for "getting mean."

A discipline misconception: If a parent later changes her discipline because of an overreaction ("I'm tired of picking up your wet towels. From now on you will dry off with toilet paper"), she risks being inconsistent or erratic. Not always so. True inconsistency is fueled by many factors: guilt, fatigue, forgetfulness, yielding to pressure from a child or others. These are "irrational" reasons that shape lax or meandering discipline.

Rationally rethinking one's discipline ("OK, you can dry off with paper towels") is a sign of parental confidence, a willingness to admit fault. And that is not inconsistency.

Further, every so often lessening a discipline consequence or its duration because a child has shown the maturity to accept it without resistance or sourness is also no sign of parental weakness. It is a sign of mercy. And mercy is not inconsistency.

CHAPTER 25

Not on Drugs

Actors: Dad; sixteen-year-old Walker
Scene: In the car
Time: After ball practice

PROLOGUE

In deciding when to allow a privilege, age is not the main factor; a child's character is. And character is measured not by the absence of problems but by the presence of virtue.

Dr. Ray: The conversation is in progress, having begun seconds after Walker fastened his passenger side seatbelt while watching his friends get into their own cars on the driver's side.

Walker: When will I be able to drive then? I'm sixteen, and all my friends have had their licenses for a while now.

Dad: We've been over this before, Walker. The fact that you're sixteen is not how we decide. Sixteen is just the minimum age that the state says you can drive a car. It's not the age at which it has to happen. Mom and I decide when you're old enough to drive, not the state. And we base that on your attitude and your maturity.

Dr. Ray: When kids are enlightening parents as to how badly out of touch they are with the mainstream, they like to cite "all" or "everyone" as the comparison group. Not that it matters, but a parent can be assured that there are "friends' parents" out there as throwback as he is. When a youngster says "everyone," he means "everyone who agrees with me."

Kids live by the numbers: I'm eighteen, so I can do what I want; I'm sixteen, so I can drive; I'm ten, so I can have a sleepover; I'm four, so I can have a cell phone. OK, maybe this one's closer to "I'm seven."

In adding to a youngster's social freedom, numbers are not the guide. Moral maturity is.

Walker: How old will I have to be? I can't see what I'm doing so wrong that I can't drive.

Dad: Well, for one thing, you know that your grades last year and so far this year have not been what they could be. All of your teachers, except in math, have told us you could do better. School is your number one responsibility, and you're not giving it your best. That's a big part of whether you get to drive or not.

Walker: My grades aren't that bad, and they came up over these nine weeks. And I never get into any trouble at school, ever, like some of my friends do. But I guess that doesn't make any difference. Sometimes I think, "What's the use? It doesn't do me any good anyway."

Dr. Ray: Walker doesn't realize it, but he's arguing against himself. One, if some of his friends get into trouble, Mom and Dad had better reassess who his friends are. And two, if Walker's main reason for "being good" is to earn perks, he hasn't yet grasped the real reasons for being good.

Yes, no "trouble" at school—if you don't count weak grades—is a good mark, but it doesn't offset bad marks. That's a bit like saying, "All right, so my room's trashed, but I brush my teeth regularly."

Dad: No, Walker, your behaving at school does make a big difference. It's one sign of character. But it's not the only one. Your teachers like you—they tell us that—but that doesn't change the fact that you've put minimal effort into your schoolwork.

Walker: You and Mom expect me to be perfect. I have nice friends; I mow four lawns; I help out around the house. It's not like I'm on drugs or anything.

Dad: We don't expect you to be perfect. But we do expect your best. And putting a three-thousand-pound vehicle under you is a major decision. We'll make it when we see a more consistent effort on your part.

Dr. Ray: A wise parent does expect a child to be perfect, if *perfect* means attaining definite standards. Is it wanting too much for siblings always to act right toward one another, or should a parent allow one punch and two insults per week, so as not to set the bar too high? No trash Internet, period, or one hour of vile sites per month? Make your bed *every* day, or on Sundays, Wednesdays, and Fridays?

Of course, perfect behavior can't be reached, but by definition, any clear standard is a perfect one. If Walker is capable of As and Bs, is it expecting perfection to expect him to achieve that?

"I'm not on drugs or anything"—one of the new moral standards out there. Said another way, "You should be grateful. I could be a lot worse." Sadly, many parents seem satisfied with this modern cultural norm. After telling me all her teen troubles, a parent often will follow with, "I think I'm giving you the wrong impression. Overall, he's a pretty good kid. He's not on drugs or anything like that."

Character is not the absence of negatives. It is the presence of positives.

Walker: Avis got to drive when she was sixteen.

Dad: Yes, she did. And she earned that privilege with her behavior.
Walker: Oh, yeah, I'm not as grown-up as Avis. She's the good one.
Dr. Ray: Parents have to stand strong against this kind of emotional blackmail. Resist being manipulated by accusations of unfairness or, worse, favoritism. Know that all privileges and freedoms are based first upon your judgment of a youngster's trustworthiness. They are not based first upon chronology.

Some of my children took a driver's test within their sixteenth year. Others will get their permits when they retire—assuming they're still living at home.

EPILOGUE

Dad's line of reasoning sounds perfectly reasonable—to grown-up ears. It falls hard on most teen ears. Not that they can't conform to it. A few somewhere deep inside might even understand it. They just don't like it or agree with it.

Does that mean a parent should never re-explain himself? No. Ever so slowly, over years, we strive to get our children to see parenting through our eyes, and most do, if only after trying to reason with their own kids. Dad made a valiant effort to answer Walker's teen-minded clichés. And for this trip, it sounds as if he got nowhere. Still, with a few more trips, he might reach Walker. I'm saying "might."

At some point, though, a reasonable parent quits reasoning, especially if arguments arrive with each go-round. When any contested issue returns—be it driving, dating, computer, cell phone, movies, friends, curfew—the parent decides how soon to end the dialogue. Walker's dad could close with, "Walker, it's pretty simple. Your grades come up, you show more cooperation, and driving becomes an option." Then, to punctuate the sentence, Dad can give Walker a blank look, as if to say, "There's not much more to say."

As a father of ten, four to six of whom have been teens at any given time, I've spent years with a blank look plastered on my face. My wife says I perfected it in the early days of our marriage.

To relate more closely to a teen's level, a parent could respond, "I like your thinking. I've never been in jail. My friends are nice people. I work real hard around here. And I'm not on drugs or anything like that."

ABOUT THE AUTHOR

Dr. Ray Guarendi is the father of ten, clinical psychologist, author, public speaker, and nationally syndicated radio host. His radio show, *The Doctor Is In,* can be heard weekdays on Ave Maria Radio, EWTN, and SiriusXM. Dr. Ray also hosts his own national television show, *Living Right With Dr. Ray.* He has been a regular guest on national radio and television, including *Oprah, The 700 Club,* and *CBS This Morning.* His first book, *You're a Better Parent Than You Think!,* is now in its twenty-eighth printing. Other books include *Discipline That Lasts a Lifetime; Good Discipline, Great Teens; Adoption: Choosing It, Living It, Loving It;* and *Marriage: Small Steps, Big Rewards.*